THE LIE CALLED CANCER

A DIVINE COMEDY

ALAN SEARLE

The Lie Called Cancer: A Divine Comedy

Published by Alan Searle Media in the United Kingdom for worldwide distribution, to glorify Christ through creative writing and truthful testimony. Online at http://alansearle.media

Some material in this book was adapted from essays published online at Pleasant Lines: https://alansearle.media. You can read cool stuff there for free, and also buy my first book.

Some people's names were changed. They will undoubtedly be grateful.

The author is responsible for any factual errors in the text. Emphasis by underlining is made by the author in some cases. All photographs by the author.

Cover by Teddi Black and Interior Design by Megan McCullough. Visit http://teddiblack.com

ISBN: 978-1-8380446-1-9
Ebook ISBN: 978-1-8380446-0-2

This book is dedicated with much love to the Faithful Pray-ers: Christa-Maria Sanders, Daniel Herring, Gaëtan Dennemont, Irene Grainger, Jessie Boston, Melanie Searle, Susannah Wynne and the Reverend Tim Jones.

Also to Alex, Anne, Beth, Bex, Catherine C., Catherine Q., Corey, Daniel, Dave, David, Debbie, Elaine, Gail, Gary, Geert, Geoffrey, Jackie, Jago, James, Jamie, Janet, Joey, Joshua, Kathy, Kit, Laurice, Leanne, Lesley, Mary, Mary Alice, Matt, Mia, Miriam, Mollie, Myrtle, Newell, Pamela, Peggy, Rachel, Ros, Rosie, Rozi, Ruth, Sam, Samson, Sandy, Sarah, Steve, Tami, Tim, Thomas, Tom, Voldemar, and everyone else who prayed in Jesus' name, including unnamed teammates at the Healing Rooms of SW London, and my lovely #BRRG family around the world.

You are all more powerful than you can imagine.

In fact, Jesus says so right here in John 14.13-14: 'I will do whatever you ask in My name, that the Father may be glorified in the Son. If you ask anything in My name, I will do it.'

And again here: 'Ask and it will be given to you; seek and you will find; knock and it will be opened to you. For everyone who asks receives, and he who seeks finds, and to him who knocks, it will be opened.' (Matthew 7.7-8)

And again here: 'Therefore I say to you, whatever things you ask when you pray, believe that you will receive them, and you will have them.' (Mark 11.24)

Finally, consider what the Lord's brother said when he got in on the act: 'The earnest prayer of a righteous person has great power and produces wonderful results.' (James 5.16, NLT)

Imagine that. You asked, God heard you, and He answered.

Author's Note

I almost titled this book 'The *Joke* Called Cancer' but thought that might offend you if you've lost a loved one to this horrible disease. If that's the case, I stand with you in your grief. No one should die from cancer. It's a scourge from hell.

Despite that, I had to write this book (mostly) as light-hearted comedy. I didn't always find laughs during my journey, but the moments without joy were rare, even in the midst of terror and despair.

I was also tempted to title it 'Cancer Is a Lie From The Devil And We Laugh At Him.' But I figured that would turn you off if you don't believe in the devil.* You might even have questioned my sanity. So that was out. Not that I'm concerned anyone think I'm dotty. You're free to do so; it's your prerogative, since you bought the book.

The Lie Called Cancer is provocative enough. Writing a book about lies may be unremarkable, because lies are so commonplace. We all lie, and it's easy to conclude that lies consume the world: consider our politics, our work, mass media, fake news, much literature, too many relationships, the delusion that those jeans actually *don't* make your butt look fat.†

Like lies, cancer is also commonplace. Unlike a lie, cancer frightens people. You say the word 'cancer' and ears prick up; heads turn. It gets attention. Putting the word 'cancer' in a book title is smart marketing.

Thanks for agreeing with me on that, and buying this book.

---

* There are way too many of you.

† In my experience, it's never the jeans, its always the Ben and Jerry's.

Foreword

This book may not be for you. That's because we'll talk a lot about my penis, my bladder, urination, and a bit about defecation and other cringe-worthy topics.* A truthful tale about bladder† cancer is like that. To mangle an aphorism, if you can't stand the heat, stay out of the loo.

On the other hand, this book may be for you, because you need a laugh and want to be uplifted in these wretched times. The book has a happy ending, after all. Whoops. I forgot your spoiler alert warning there! Too bad.

There are many things in this story that can't be explained other than to say God did it. I can't claim it was all coincidence. Remember, truth is always stranger than fiction. You may actually think that parts of this story are downright weird, even though they are all true.

I agree with you. But there's an excellent reason for the weirdness. It's because God is weird. He's really weird. He's like, beyond anyone's comprehension weird. He's shake your head in disbelief and fire up Netflix to binge on *Stranger Things* weird.

Seriously, have you actually read the Bible? Donkeys talking, axe heads floating, the sun standing still, men running faster then horses. God even comes to earth as a man. People are raised from the dead. Your sins are forgiven.

Speaking of *stranger things*...

But don't worry. Modern medicine is weird too. Really weird. It's shake your head in disbelief and fire up Netflix to binge on *House* weird. That's because it's all about the body.

* Prostate alert!

† I just think the word 'bladder' itself is amusing. Say it aloud ten times and see if you agree. Get a toddler to say it ten times. Amusing is good, because this book is meant to induce laughter and we'll say 'bladder' together a lot in the coming pages.

And raw biology is often quick to turn heads. And stomachs. Medicine may be weird, but the people who practice it definitely are not. They are lovely. Every last one of them.

I'm immensely indebted to all the physicians, nurses, assistants, specialists, technicians, receptionists, administrators, runners, cleaners and volunteers who toil so lovingly and devotedly in Britain's National Health Service (NHS), particularly at Kings College and Guy's Hospitals, and most especially at Guys' Cancer-Free Centre.

You cannot be praised enough.

Too often when I offered a compliment, you'd respond with typical British modesty, saying, 'Well, I try!'

I'm here to say with unbridled American enthusiasm: 'You succeed!'

About This Book

This book is written chronologically from my personal journals between April 2019 and April 2020. The chapter headings are the dates of the journal entries. So, if you watch the chapter headings perspicaciously,* you won't get lost.

The idea for this book arrived in late January 2020, after which I began assembling notes and writing an outline. Fast and furious scrivening† began in early February. My goal was to finish all but the final chapter by 24 April, when I was originally scheduled for a post-treatment consultation.

The plan was to immediately go home after that conversation, write the happy ending to this book, and publish it. We'll just see how that worked out.

Alan Searle
London, United Kingdom
25 May, 2020

* 'Perspicaciously' means acutely, or with penetrating mental discernment. That's you, Dear Reader. And, I promise not to drop any more five syllable words on you, unless they are medical terms.

† This is a nod to Aunt Sandy, who's the only one who won't want to redact the joke.

How to Use This Book

Simply enough, you just turn from one page to the next until you're done.

Then you go to my website (https://alansearle.media) and sign up for my newsletter because you can't wait to find out more about what I'm writing next.

There are many footnotes in this book, some relevant, and some annoying. This is where many of the jokes reside. My wife Melanie thinks I overdid the footnotes, particularly in my Ameri-centric dissection of the oddities of British culture and use of the language. I assured her these notes are meant to be deliberately aggravating.*

She also recently commented incredulously† about a book she read that had two Forewords, a Preface *and* an Introduction.

So, I added this extra section to be annoying to her. I succeed at that so rarely.

She's a saint like that.

* You'll find British usage throughout this book because it makes me look more intellectual. Also, my UK spell check prefers UK English. Also also, as I now live in the UK, I should, out of respect, learn the language. I *have* mastered saying 'SHED-jule' for 'SKED-jul' and 'PROH-gress' for 'PRAH-gress' (which makes me sound to my American ears like I'm a Canadian), but I'll be durned if I can say 'GARE-udge' without feeling exceedingly self-conscious.

† Okay, so I lied about the five syllable thing.

PART ONE:

ARREST

5 February, 2020

Before we begin, I want you to know a few things about me. Above all else, I'm a person who seeks to live in a state of unbounded joy. I'd like to believe that Bliss is my middle name. If there's a cloud, I search for the silver lining. If there's a pile of manure, that means there's a pony around here somewhere. There is no downside, ever. Well, not quite.

The truth is that all these attitudes were challenged greatly during the year covered in this book, and I uncovered some that were not so savoury. I faced direct threats to my life, my physical health, my emotional well-being and my spiritual underpinnings. There were times when my compass needle spun wildly.

I do talk about God a bit in this book, because I believe in Him, and He plays more than a big part in the story. If you're a Christian, you'll be okay with this (probably). If not, you'll happily find that I quote Scripture as little as possible. You may be uninterested in it, and I can't effectively evangelise in a book like this anyway. Invite me for drinks instead; we'll tackle it there. You can leave when you are truly pissed (take that either way).

There is *some* discussion of Scripture, but only to give you a better idea of where I'm coming from. You can pretend those bits are the Russian names in The Brothers Karamazov if you like. Just blink past them. If you don't believe in 'supernatural' stuff, but still want to enjoy this book, you get to overlook a few things. It might be easier than you think.

Here's how. You may already want to believe in a Harry Potter universe (because Riddikulus, or more practically, Accio!) or the Cthuhlu Mythos, so why not give this a shot? It's no weirder than those are. And, in fairness, while I don't believe in Harry Potter's magic myself, it doesn't mean I can't enjoy the literature. You'll live, and you'll laugh. You only have to wade through a few paragraphs anyway. Here are two of them.

God is good. That's theology 101. He also involves Himself in my daily affairs to the extent I invite Him to do so. I believe in things supernatural and prophetic, and I know that God has spoken to me (and others, on my behalf) many times. This is my normal. So don't be surprised when this pops up in the story.

Because of that Christian bit, I fully believe that the prayers of many people were instrumental in my resistance to side-effects and ultimately to the health I enjoy today. Without prayer, I believe things would have turned out for the worse if not the worst.

In fact, it's all in my medical record! If you like, I'll send you a copy (you pay outrageous shipping and handling). Regarding all the above, I don't need to explain something in order to believe it's true. You can't explain how you think, but are certain that you do. Or think you do, anyway.

Next, while this book is ostensibly about treatment for cancer, it's moreover a story about my spiritual healing. The psychological effects of receiving a cancer diagnosis and the rigours of cancer treatment are understandably severe. Living through them while *thriving joyfully* must have been God's doing. It wasn't mine.

Finally, I believe two other things: As of this writing, 5 February 2020, I'm free from cancer, and I'll live the rest of my life without it troubling me again. The doctors haven't caught up with the first part – I'm not due in the CT and MRI suites until mid-April 2020, some eight or nine weeks from this writing. As for the second part, only God knows, but I trust Him.

Those are all the things I want you to know about me. Here are the things doctors would want you to know about me: I'm a 63 year old white American male of British extraction, a former cigarette smoker (40 years) with some cancer in my family history. The medics are not surprised to see me.

---

6 February, 2020

Every so often, now that it's over, I like to revisit the scene of the crime. Let's look back 41 weeks ago.

---

18 April, 2019

The scene is a certain urinal in a certain South London supermarket. The crime was the appearance of a blood clot the size of a pea. Life did a full stop for a few beats as I stared at it, astonished that such a thing should fall out of my body. Bright red, it contrasted sharply against the fresh white porcelain. For a moment I imagined it pulsing with a life of its own, ready to snarl, turn viciously and attack. I stepped away feeling violated.

'Babe,' I said, rejoining my wife in the aisles. 'We need to head to the GP now, and put off the shopping until tomorrow.' Melanie looked puzzled, but only until I explained. Then it was her turn to have life do a full stop for a few beats. We abandoned the shopping and headed out.

It was the Thursday before Easter, and my surgery* was about to close for four days. They squeezed me in for a quick consultation. I left a sample in a bottle (results not to be known for a week due to the holiday). Dr. Kuracisto gave me a course of antibiotic 'in case its just a urinary tract infection.'

Well, it wasn't that. It eventually turned out to be bigger than that. It was a crime, and the crime was a lie. It was the lie called cancer.

---

19 April, 2019

I didn't know it was supposed to be a cancer then, of course. It was way too early to think seriously about cancer anyway, and I didn't. The blood could be from many causes. Until I had more information, there was nothing to do but wait.

It's so easy to think worst-case when something happens to my body, especially with a vivid imagination like mine. That pain in my knee? Could be an inflammation. If it's inflammation, it might be arthritis. In fact, it probably *is* arthritis. Arthritis is incurable and untreatable. It's probably rheumatoid arthritis. My mum had that, and it can be inherited. So, for sure, that's it.

Before long I have myself so crippled in my mind I'm ready to shop for a wheelchair and a van with a lift. You never know how soon I might need one, right? Best to be prepared! Why do I automatically think worst-case about my body? Well, it's not like I can quickly whip out a list of *best-case* items when blood-

---

* 'Surgery' is *doctor's office* to my American readers. It's also, according to the Cambridge Dictionary, 'the regular period of time when a person can visit their Member of Parliament to ask advice.' I'll refrain from making any cutting political remarks.

in-the-urine is involved. I've thought about that for almost a year now, and I still don't have item #1.

Faced with a potentially scary track ahead, my train of thought derails immediately, instead of pulling into a bright shiny station with free coffee and helpful baggage handlers. Those noisy worst-case scenarios always shove to the front of the queue, waving their First Class tickets, ready to ride my train all the way to the last stop.

Let's face it, even a ridiculously optimistic person like me sometimes has to throw in the towel and conclude the only positive aspect of the situation is that I had an extra towel to begin with. But I'd ride that train to the last stop as well. I had no choice.

---

22 April, 2019

It's an odd sensation to stand before a toilet and wonder what's about to come out. It had been so easy to take urination for granted. I'd never concerned myself with it. Have you? Isn't peeing an unthinking act? Until now, my experience only involved pee. But, when you add blood, urination morphs into the fancy Greek medical term haematuria.

Now that I was focused on the bleeding, I also became aware of some discomfort during the act itself. The discomfort was probably there before the previous Thursday's display made it all obvious, but I hadn't noticed. If I had, my trip to the GP would have happened much earlier, I suppose. But I didn't. And so, here we are.

In the absence of information, how to proceed? Step one for me always should be to pray. That's what Christians learn. It's supposed to be automatic, like gently turning *into* a skid when your car fishtails. I constantly surprise myself at how often prayer is *not* my first choice. I turn away from the skid more often than I care to admit.

Then, when I do finally get around to prayer, I must remember that not all prayers are created equal. True prayer involves surrender to God's will. Anything else is a demand. Let me give you a little Theology 101 about that. Only a couple of paragraphs. Hang in there.

I'll start here: it's inarguable to me that God is good, 100 percent. If not, why believe in Him? Evil is not from God. It's either caused by the devil, is influenced by the devil, or results from my own sin. The Bible reveals this repeatedly from the first page to the last.

Because God is good, he couldn't have created cancer, or any other illness for that matter, your love of the book of Job notwithstanding. End of Theology 101. If you aren't a Christian, you now have a pivotal choice.

You can take my word for all this and keep reading (your best option IMHO*). Or, you can study the Bible for yourself to see if it's true and then come back. I'll see you in a few months – you'll need to be thorough. Or, you can put the book down, say it was a bad investment and go read *Harry Potter and the Cursed Child* for the third time.

If you care to know more about why I believe these things, you can read my memoir, Masterpiece (A Love Story), which is available through Amazon. Yeah, I know – its a shameless plug. But hey – I'm an author, and I sell books to put bread on the table. Or into the bank account, as the case may be.

---

* In My Holy Opinion

30 April, 2019

The antibiotics came and went, but the symptoms remained, and the test was negative – no Urinary Tract Infection (UTI). I found myself back in Dr. Kuracisto's office.

'How do you feel?' (This is Standard Doctor Question #4).

'It still hurts when I pee and sometimes blood comes out. Otherwise, I'm just chuffed!'

'Well you definitely don't have a UTI, but there is something amiss in there.' He reached for some gloves.

'Pull down your trousers and lean against the bed,' he said. Dr. Kuracisto stepped into his phone booth and burst out as Professor Jellyfinger. During rectal exams I can't help but wonder, did I wipe well enough? And, how do they teach that in medical school? The probing is rude but not outrageously uncomfortable. It's mercifully short.

'Your prostate is slightly enlarged but that's not unusual for a man your age. That's good news. I'll write a referral to the Urology Department at Kings Hospital,' he said. 'It's on a fast track, so you should hear from them in a few days.'

NHS prioritises well, to the dismay of some patients who are forced to wait for minor operations.* If a GP suspects cancer, a case is automatically on 'fast track.'

'What will happen over there?' I asked.

'They'll likely give you a cystoscopy. That's an internal examination of your bladder, to see what's going on.'

Well, let me just look that up. According to NHS documentation, the procedure available to me as an outpatient is called a 'flexible cystoscopy.' This device has a camera and a light on the end, and a tube that allows water in and out. It's about as big around as a pencil.

---

* I had been an exception to this earlier in the year. Details (and another grody medical story) to be found in the entry for 22 May, 2019.

The cystoscope is inserted in the urethra, which is the tube that allows urine to pass out of the body. The urethra is *not* as big around as a pencil. It's about as big around as the stem of a Q-tip. Read 'inserted into the urethra' as '*inserted into the penis*.' No man wants to hear about this, much less contemplate it. Yes, ladies, I'm certain this procedure is just as physically disturbing for you as for us. But for me, as a man, it's also an assault on my ego. Just sayin'.

---

1 May, 2019

Okay – so now I had some information. It appeared that life was about to get more painful. Much more painful. I waited as patiently as possible, only occasionally drumming my fingers on the table in frustration. My main occupation had to be prayer, *doing nothing* about any of this (as though I could). That's easier said than done sometimes.

(Insert big self-piteous Christian sigh here)

It's exceedingly tough to sit tight while my head yells at me about doom and destruction, such as the eventual need to buy that wheelchair van. I'll give you a few examples, but only because I'm certain this *never* happens to you: official mail is automatically bad news; being called into the head office means I'm sacked; my candidate will always lose the election; it's not only cancer, but *terminal* cancer, so pick the bouquets for the memorial service now!

I had to repeatedly remind myself I knew nothing, and shouldn't decide pre-emptively on something as 'the truth'. All I knew with certainty was that there was blood in my urine. Inventing a reason for it would be mindless speculation.

There's no truth there, only mindlessness. Speculation leads me to fear, which makes me lose my bearings. Such feelings aren't a signpost. They are paint thrown on the signpost so I cannot find the way.

My only choice was to respond through surrender. I kept in front of me the only truth I had, tiny slice though it was: the bleeding was from an unknown cause. Yes, there was an answer, but it hadn't arrived yet. Like many things in the Christian life, the way forward was simple. Wait, rest and pray. I wished I was better at them.

---

4 May, 2019

It's our wedding anniversary, so Melanie and I enjoyed a short walking holiday in the New Forest, which is a very odd name for an area that's been actively managed since 1079 AD. I haven't located the Old Forest yet. Possibly it was felled to feed the Industrial Revolution.

One of the joys of a malfunctioning bladder is scouting for every available toilet within one's range (while carrying hope for some that don't actually exist). This is done continually during travel. Fortunately, I'm endowed with male equipment. This means the world is my urinal, so long as privacy can be assured (yours, not mine – I'm not afflicted with body modesty). To my knowledge, no local water quality was affected by these necessary escapades.

It's a month to the day before I'll check into the Day Surgery* unit at Kings College Hospital in London. I was still

* Not a member of Parliament in sight

unaware of this procedure as we traipsed through the woods of Wiltshire, but it's useful to talk about it here.

The operation is called a TURBT, which has nothing to do with the fish. The acronym stands for Trans-Urethral Resection of a Bladder Tumour. That's doctor-speak for 'we'll shove yet another oversized tool up yours and carve out a few bits with great hope that we don't puncture anything.' During research for this book (yes, I actually did research; all facts are purportedly true) I discovered that the cost of a TURBT varies widely, depending on the provider, and where in the world it's done.

An item published by European Urology* reports that a TURBT in the United States can cost anywhere between $3,000 and $6,000 depending on whether it's an outpatient or inpatient procedure. Some other parts of the world have less expensive options, some more so.

You probably are unsurprised that there are internet forums on bladder cancer, as with everything else. I declined to engage with them before writing this book, mostly because they're full of speculation and negative declaration. That's Christian-speak for what your therapist and Oprah Winfrey would refer to as 'negative self-talk.' Whatever you call it, it's bad for you, so knock it off, right now. I avoid both as assiduously as I do five-syllable words.

There was an item on one forum, for example, where a person reported being billed $12,950 for a TURBT, itemised† nicely among the Anaesthesiologist, the outpatient department,

* https://www.europeanurology.com/article/S0302-2838(14)00018-9/fulltext/the-economics-of-bladder-cancer-costs-and-considerations-of-caring-for-this-disease

† Another fun game for my American readers, 'Count the Esses'. The British apparently place a premium on the letter zed (that's 'z' to you) and use it as little as possible. Thus, many words you might end with an -ize, the British end with -ise. They get stroppy (that's snotty, to you) when you question them about this, possibly because they claim to have invented the language. The British haven't outlawed zed yet, but it's not invited to many parties. A typically eccentric rule. Itemized isn't okay, but sized and squeezed pass muster. Prized does too, unless it's the verb meaning to force something open, in which case it is prised. It's hard to stay apprised of these things, but 'I try,' (he said with typical British modesty).

the Urologist (who was presumably the surgeon) and the Pathologist. The latter, being the geekiest, only copped $150 off the deal.

That cost, $12,950, was reported *ten years ago*. An extrapolation from US Centers for Disease Control data suggests that the cost of that same TURBT five years later would've been just over $16,000. I'd guess that it might be close to twenty grand today, at the same rate of increase.

Finding consistent medical cost data beyond 2015 is a challenge, at least for someone like me who's only willing to do cursory research for a book of this type. I've concluded that only God's own accountant could possibly know what any health care anywhere in the world actually costs.

All this meandering brings me to my actual point.

That point is that I'm truly blessed to be in the United Kingdom for this portion of My Personal Health Care Journey. When I applied to enter Britain on a Spousal Visa in 2018, I paid a £1,000 'immigration health surcharge', giving me full access to the National Health Service. This amounts to £400 per year over the life of my visa – an incredible bargain. Thank you Aneurin Bevan.

I don't believe anyone at NHS is aware of what anything costs either. Until Her Majesty's Government finds it prudent to do a wide-scale review of how NHS operates (which hasn't been done since it was founded 70 years ago), who could know? What's more, I suspect if anyone at NHS tried to call out the figures, they wouldn't be heard over the giant sucking sound made by 7% of the British Gross Domestic Product (GDP) being hoovered* away to keep us all healthy and alive despite our best attempts to be otherwise (pass me some smokes and another pint of bitter, mate).

Even with top-level insurance in the States, I'd shell out thousands upon thousands in co-pays for this care. And that's

* 'Hoover' is the British word for the household vacuum. Not to be mis-used by speaking of outer space as a 'near total hoover.'

just the TURBT. We haven't even gotten to the stars of the show yet. This is only the warm-up act.

I've read many heart-rending stories of American bladder cancer patients who were forced to piss away (no pun intended) their life savings, or take impossibly-large personal loans, to afford the treatment they needed. Suffice it to say, this thing would have rendered me bankrupt several times over.

But, I'm not in the States any more. God moved me across The Pond for many reasons, and apparently free medical treatment was one of them.*

A final note for those of you scoring at home. 7% of the British GDP amounts to £134 billion. That's enough to buy 255,238,095 used Russian cystoscopes through E-bay (see next entry).

---

11 May, 2019

OK, so I lied. I'm not really going to talk about cystoscopes just yet. That happens in the *next* entry. No, really. I will talk about them – I promise. And I'm willing to wait while you flip ahead and check if you don't believe me. See? I was telling the truth. This time.

Back to the story. We were now home from our lovely anniversary holiday (where I spent inordinate amounts of time playing with my zip), and I suspected it was my last free weekend for a while. I was about to become intimate with medical professionals who were about to become intimate with me.

This wasn't like the Dating Game or Bachelorette. No one in my world was about to get happy after a couple of short and

---

* This gives me yet another opportunity for yet another shameless plug of my previous memoir, Masterpiece (A Love Story), available on Amazon, where that part of my history is told. Caveat emptor: that book is not funny like this one. You will either throw it away in disgust or have a good cry over it.

contrived episodes. Instead, it was time to play my favourite game, called 'What Do I Know?'

- It hurts when I wee* and sometimes, blood clots come out
- I'm being internally examined this week to get the lie of the land
- Odds are good there's surgery coming, but I have no idea what it is

Oh, a lot more information was available, if I wanted to get on the internet. But then I'd have to play 'What Do I Speculate?', a game that never ends well, psychologically or emotionally. Speculation is Not Good. It leads to anxiety and worry and ultimately, fear. The Bible says that God hasn't given me the spirit of fear, but of power, and love, and self-control. I work at this.† Self-control includes me not looking things up on the internet. This type of self-control is a very good thing for anyone with an as-yet-undiagnosed medical condition.

We've already reviewed my alarming propensity for blowing things out of proportion, which brings us back to Theology 101. I'm not a fan of praying weakly in supplication, hoping God might actually pay attention. No, I prefer to say things that *get His attention*, meaning things He's already said. So I say things like, 'Death and life are in the power of the tongue, and those who love it will eat its fruit'‡

That's a fancy way of saying that *I say what I believe and I believe what I say*. So I'd better put things in my inner being that benefit me when they eventually come out. Here's an example. For years I've routinely thanked God aloud for giving me a strong, healthy body and a powerful immune system that rejects sickness and disease.

---

* English for pee, Scots for tiny. No comment from Wales – its too busy winning at Six Nations Rugby.

† 1 Tim 1:7

‡ Proverbs 18:20

Just as regular workouts build muscle, these declarations have built faith. After all, what *do* I want to believe? That I'm strong and healthy? Or, that I'm sickly and weak? What's my final word on the subject?

When someone warns me off from a handshake or getting too close, I'll take their hand, or hug them anyway, saying, 'It's okay – I don't get sick.' I generally don't. On the rare occasions when I'm attacked by cold or flu symptoms, I don't take to my bed, or complain. I refuse to declare that I'm sick. Instead I stare those little suckers right in the eye and rebuke them repeatedly, until they go away. It works.

Others around me will be dropping like flies, ill for a week, two weeks, a month, bemoaning their fate. I'll have a day or two of discomfort, and then it's over. A friend came up to me a couple years ago, sneezing and sniffling and complaining. 'I don't know how I caught this cold,' he said. Before I could stop myself, I asked, 'Why did you have your hands out?'

Prayer is warfare. I must be well-armed. Those who don't recognize this are left unprotected on the battlefield. You try to hand me a cancer diagnosis? In the timeless words of Bugs Bunny, 'Of course you know, this means war!' *

The battle was about to begin.

---

14 May, 2019 (Morning)

Relax. The eye-wateringly hilarious cystoscope business is almost here. Comic relief is finally in sight.

I'd been living with some small discomfort before the crime occurred, but like the frog in the pot, hadn't really noticed. You

* Also uttered less menacingly by Groucho Marx in 'A Night at the Opera.'

know about the frog in the pot? When it's dropped into hot water, it gets out immediately – it's too hot! Put it in cold water, heat it up gradually, and Froggy only feels hot after it's too late.

Now that I was bleeding regularly, it hurt full time. A lot. Peeing can be a relief, in fact it's called 'relieving oneself' for a reason. Now, it was only a relief for me when it was over. I had pain, and also greater pain. When the greater pain had passed, it was back to pain. What began as a two on a scale of ten had ramped up to about a five. When I emptied my bladder, it was closer to an eight. I have a pretty good tolerance for pain and my personal rating of ten on the pain scale means I'm crying. If it went beyond that, I'd likely pass out (I've been understandably reluctant to try this). I count an eight as 'Wincing'.

To get the terminology right, I'll walk you all the way from one to ten. We begin with Denial and a couple levels of Discomfort, moving quickly through This Too Shall Pass (no pun intended). That's followed directly by Nuisance, Trouble and Sweating. After a deep breath, we come to Wincing (level eight), and then Wailing and finally, Weeping.

I'll admit to having reached Ten more than once in my life, and I don't recommend it, just in case you are eager to masochistically check your own scale against mine.

My fast track had taken me in less than three weeks to the day unit at Kings College Hospital in London. I was scheduled for Baby's First Cystoscopy. The office was clean and well-appointed, and like most NHS facilities of my acquaintance it was also well-used. Not *shabby* exactly, but with an air of age. Maybe that's just Britain. After all, the country has more than 1,500 years of *written* history.

Kings itself opened in 1840 and is old enough that Joseph Lister performed the world's first truly antiseptic surgery there. Lister was an international superstar in 1879 and yes, Listerine was named after him. According to the book Freakonomics, Listerine was originally developed as an antiseptic but was also variously marketed as a floor cleaner and a cure for gonorrhoea, before settling in as America's best-known mouthwash.

Most NHS waiting rooms are not like American waiting rooms. Thankfully, there was no TV blaring Telemundo soap operas or a politically-slanted cable news channel. I'm glad I had something to read, because there were no magazines either. This isn't an issue for the British. They are enthusiastic readers and carry their reading with them, possibly because most of what's on the telly is rubbish. Happily, the UK still has a thriving newspaper industry, potentially serving millions of birdcages and fish and chips customers weekly. Barring that, the Brits will carp endlessly about the weather, just like Oregonians.

The atmosphere was casually businesslike, and no one was in a hurry. Being a urology office, most of those waiting were older, and generally ignored one another. Periodically, a patient came along in a wheelchair. My name was called, and I met Angel #1, a Bahamian-born nurse who clearly had seen it all during her 28 years on that ward. She was bright and cheery and prone to joking. She handed me a vial, which I was to fill and return to her.

'I'm almost out of funnels right now and so got to save them for the ladies, so be careful and don't spill!'

I complied and returned a sample, complete with three tiny blood clots. Eventually, my name was called a second time, and I strode bravely into the face of the unknown. Or, as it happened, wandered meekly and uncertainly down the corridor to Examination Room Five.

Before I knew it, I was splayed out on an examination table in that small room tucked away at the back of the unit. There was just enough space beyond the exam table for a rolling stand with electronic equipment, topped by a very large video monitor on a swinging arm. A small metal side table had the cystoscope laid out on it. The room was hot and stuffy.

The scope's camera eye stared menacingly as I lay there helpless, soon to be naked from the waist down in front of God knows who. The light at the tip pulsed rapidly, possibly to ensure I had a high enough blood pressure. The flexible cystoscope is described in the literature as 'bendy.' Lying on the table it didn't *look* flexible, although it had to be: my inward parts twist and turn, so it must too.

It resembled nothing more than a giant syringe, except in place of a needle was a way-too-long probe. The very word 'probe' makes me shudder because it can so easily be wielded as a verb. In my mind's eye the thing resembled a big wooden dowel or possibly a curtain rod. I didn't ask if it was new or used, or if it came direct from the manufacturer, or if they found it on Ebay. Or how they might sterilise it.

Dr. Gvidi squeezed in with the nurse, Angel #2. Two more bodies suddenly made the airless cubicle even warmer and more humid. I heard Han Solo in my head saying, 'I've got a bad feeling about this!'

A couple entries back I mentioned a Q-tip. That mention was a hip literary device called 'foreshadowing.' You get bonus points if you find the other foreshadowing scattered throughout this book. But I digress (another hip literary device). As the moment of his First Cystoscopy became imminent, Baby was now Sweating, waiting for Wincing. The video monitor was conveniently placed so I wouldn't miss a thing.

The tiny nature of the exam room made the screen look like the JumboTron® at Madison Square Garden, or possibly an IMAX® projection, thankfully not 3D. I could only avoid watching by squeezing my eyes shut, which happened periodically as the examination proceeded. Wince-level pain includes involuntary eye-squeezing. Now you know.

Documentation from the Cancer Research UK website explains that the patient may undergo some *discomfort* during the procedure. You may recall that Discomfort is only a two or three on my pain scale. Cancer Research UK stands guilty of a gross medical understatement. The local anaesthetic did all it could, which technically was Not Much, and so we began. I was unable to stop watching. The only thing worse than watching was not watching. Watching was the only shred of control remaining. Dr. Gvidi was nonchalant and relaxed and clearly received perfect scores in the 'Tour Guide' portion of his medical education.

Seriously, his narration of this journey was non-stop. It was like going to hell with a grating voice-over describing every eternal flame and torturing devil. There I was, breathing sulphurous fumes and burning up, and through it all, I would have chosen ear plugs over a fireproof suit with breathing mask. Dr. Gvidi was practically panting with interest in what was around the next corner, and happily chattered away endlessly. I began to wish that English was not his second language, or that I had the strength to gag him.

Meanwhile, I was supposed to be lulled into supposing that Angel #2's role was only to pat me reassuringly as I loudly called on Jesus. Only the Lord Himself knows now whether this was supplication or cursing on my part. However, there was no doubt that if I began to flail, or attempted to clamp the doctor's mouth shut, or tried to bolt from the room, Angel #2 would have kept me immobile. I'm sure it was an important part of her training.*

But as it happened, I was in too much shock to move, pinned there to the mat like a captured insect, staring helplessly at the video. The tour finally arrived at our destination, my bladder, after the 14-mile expedition up the urethra, through the prostate gland and past the sphincter. Several litres of water, possibly 80, were then squirted into my bladder to inflate it, making for a more entertaining video tour. Lying there as I was, I couldn't see my belly to prove it, but I felt like a woman at 39 weeks gestation.

---

* Greco-Roman wrestling anyone?

The quarry was easily found, crouching on the bladder wall like a bloody bat in its cave. Its four-centimetre nastiness hung just above the sphincter. It was a tumour, all right. Dr. Gvidi flew us around in there like a spacecraft inside a Dyson Sphere: taking pictures, mumbling arcane medical jargon (in English, I think), speculating on the nature of the tumour. He told me what I didn't want to hear: it looked like a malignant growth.

In his opinion, it looks cancerous. He added some detail, that it's 'T-2, possibly T-3', which meant it definitely had grown well into the bladder wall, and perhaps into the layer of fatty tissue beyond. T-3 tumours can be hard to treat. You don't even want to think about T-4, where the inmates have escaped the asylum altogether to romp merrily through the abdominal cavity. They create outposts elsewhere in the belly, set up shop in a lymph node, or worm their way into the prostate gland.

Dr. Gvidi didn't take a biopsy. I asked him why not. 'No biopsy?' I'm limited to short sentence fragments due to the predicted *discomfort*.

'I can't do that with this instrument,' he said. 'Even if I could, the tumour's already bleeding, so a tissue sample would only make it worse. The surgeons will do a biopsy when they remove the tumour.'

'Surgery then?'

'Oh yes, for certain.'

'We done?'

'Yes – out we come.'*

The Cancer Research UK team also advised that 'at the end of the test, you'll want to go to the toilet.' This was another gross understatement: it's not a want, it's a demand, an extremely urgent one. And, I'm here to tell you, passing 80 litres through a tube the size of a Q-tip takes a long, long time.

---

* I imagined the sound of a slide-whistle as this occurred.

14 May, 2019 (Afternoon)

I took this all home. I have a tumour in my bladder, and have been told it's partially necrotic. That's Greek for DEAD, although some types of dead are better than others. There is good necrosis and bad necrosis. When a tumour shrinks due to treatment, tissue dies and flakes off. That's good necrosis. When a tumour grows too fast, tissue dies and flakes off. That's bad necrosis, showing up in my case as blood clots in the urine.

According to the Japanese Journal of Clinical Oncology,* bad necrosis happens because the tumour outgrows its own blood supply and runs out of oxygen. It's the neoplasmic equivalent of drinking itself into a coma. My worst-case brain saw the tumour expanding exponentially, doubling in size every hour, commanding every resource my body could muster, until it ate me from the inside out. Fortunately, medical treatment can move me from bad necrosis to good necrosis, dragging me across the line from actively dying, back to merely ageing gracefully.

So, Cancer. The Big C. Cancer news sends chills down the spine for most of us. There's an expectation that it's bad, going to worsen, and the victim is in for the fight of his life. Too often, people think Cancer = Death Sentence, even though survival rates are pretty good. They cling hopefully (but barely) to survival statistics, fearing the worst.

In their secret hearts, many people, even people of faith, can't see beyond that. They see a cancer diagnosis as a condemnation, divine payback for some sin or misdeed. Cancer is like the ultimate type of bad karma. I found out later, per Cancer Research UK, that I began this journey with a 63% chance of surviving five years, and a 50-50 chance of living ten.

I dislike that word 'chance'. It's problematic; it's misdirection. It implies I have no say in the matter. Just as the world didn't

* https://academic.oup.com/jjco (accessed March 4, 2020)

randomly spring into existence out of nothing,* my living or dying is subject to more than just statistics. That's what I believe, but as you'll see, while I often talk a good game, I sometimes forget to carry the ball.

---

14 May, 2019 (Evening)

Warfare language often associated with cancer is unhelpful. Society talks about 'battling cancer', which implies cancer has a good chance of winning. Or, that I somehow fail if I'm unwell, or ultimately don't live. Likewise, 'fighting cancer' implies that losing is a huge risk.

I've read many obituaries declaring that the deceased 'lost a valiant fight' with cancer. I'm sorry for these deaths, but I don't find the idea of dying from a painful and debilitating disease in any way ennobling. It's not my place to fight, but to surrender. More about that in a moment.

'Surviving cancer' makes it sound like my survival is somehow a product of luck or coincidence (there are those statistics again).

Many people refer to cancer as 'my cancer', as though they've taken ownership of the disease. They've allowed it to change their identity. I know one man who bought a personalised car license plate that read 'Survivor.' He couldn't wait to have people ask him about it!

---

* Sorry Darwinians, you're just wrong about that. You can't have a created thing without a creator. *American Atheists* magazine doesn't spontaneously appear in your mail each month. Someone creates it. The truth that every created thing in our world has a creator can't operate in a universe that supposedly sprang out of nothing, because it obviates that truth. The universe must be subject to the same law. Otherwise, you defy the logic you claim to live by.

Sorry, friend. It's true that receiving a cancer diagnosis and getting treatment took up inordinate amounts of my 2019, and made life inconvenient at times. In retrospect, it was far from the most important thing to happen to me last year. If I weren't writing about it, I wouldn't think about it much at all.

Those of us being treated for cancer are described as 'brave', as though I and others had a choice about being treated.* Calling it 'The Big C' brings in the Bogeyman Effect, meaning that cancer is a malevolent force that's incapable of being tamed or controlled.

And then there are the day-to-day phrases, which are also unhelpful. 'Coping' implies that overcoming cancer is somehow not possible, and that I'm in a passive, powerless state. To 'deal with it' says that it's a nuisance that cannot be controlled. 'Living with cancer' tells me that it's an invited guest.

Finally, for me to say 'I have cancer' means I've taken ownership of it. I refused to do that. What's more, I'll never be told that I'm 'cured' or 'healed.' I'll be declared 'in remission.' There's no freedom in that. It keeps me captive to the idea that cancer will never go away. I'd be no healthier than the paranoiac who compulsively peeps outside to see who might be watching the house.

Even if I were to say that I 'beat cancer' there's still an assumption that somehow I was waging a battle I chose to engage in, that it was a war of my choosing. As I mentioned a moment ago, my best option wasn't to fight, but to surrender. That's the Biblical way. I can't successfully attack the devil, I can only 'stand' against him, or 'resist' him (see Ephesians 6 and 1 Peter 5).

So, to summarise: warfare words tell me nothing more than I'm afraid of cancer. I thought back to my friend suffering from a cold. 'Why did you have your hands out?' I was very determined that rainy evening after limping home

---

* I guess we actually *do* have a choice. Christian Scientists take note.

from Kings College Hospital. I'd been handed a diagnosis of cancer, and I refused to accept it. I have yet to say 'I have cancer', 'I had cancer', 'I am (or was) a cancer patient'. I would certainly never label myself a 'cancer victim.' It's definitely not 'my cancer.' But I told the truth. I told people 'I am being treated for cancer.'

Crisis provokes one of two responses in the human heart. Face up to it (surrender), or run and hide (try to control it). Here was my choice then: Either turn to the God I know and lean on Him (surrender), or turn away and blame Him for my problems (try to control it). Faith or fear. Those are my only options. Even 'wait and see' ultimately leads to one or the other.

I embraced the way of faith, and rejected fear as much as possible. My expectations had to be set by God's promises. He hadn't carried me this far to drop me now.* I'd speak His truth, even when I didn't believe it. I *am not* and *will not* be afraid, I told myself. Cancer is *not* my master. Jesus is my Master. I was confident God would carry me through this trial. I would *not* lose my joy, even when I felt unhappy or afraid. Because of God's help, I would not be powerless in my surrender.

That's all of what I want you to know. Here's what the doctors want you to know (from the official record):

It was a pleasure to see this 62-year-old gentleman as a walk-in patient at the Flexible Cystoscopy Clinic today. He has been having episodes of haematuria for the last three weeks with passage of clots. He does not have any episodes of lower urinary tract symptoms or symptoms of urinary tract infections. His grandfather had bladder tumour and he (is) an ex-smoker. He is on Levothyroxine for hypothyroidism. I have

* Yet another shameless opportunity to plug my first book, which provides context for these attitudes.

done the flexible cystoscopy and it revealed[*] *a necrotic issue (sic)*[†] *at the left UO.*[‡]

Here's the understatement I really liked (emphasis mine): *I have explained the procedure (TURBT) in detail, and possible complications like blood in the urine, catheter, damage to the bladder and bladder perforation.*

Legal bases covered, he concluded: *We would be happy to see him in Day Surgery Unit in due course for the procedure.*

I bet you would.

---

15 May, 2019

I got my picture taken today, only it's not something for social media. It's an ultrasound of my bladder. This gives the physicians a low-res black and white image to accompany the hi-def full-colour movie I posed for yesterday. As many women who have been pregnant know, these scans are done with a

---

* 'Reveal' is the excellent term the British use when they want to officially tell you something you wouldn't know otherwise. American TV and newspaper reports will say they have an 'exclusive.' In Britain they 'reveal' something or when it's really hot, 'exclusively reveal' it. Unfortunately, this has been subsumed into popular culture to become pointless and socially acceptable hyperbole. My favourite example is the popular dance contest programme, *Strictly Come Dancing.* Hosts 'exclusively reveal' to their audience which contestant is condemned to a dance-off to survive the contest another week. As though anyone outside the show's production unit would have that information? I can exclusively reveal to you I think the use of this phrase is idiotic.

† The report should read 'tissue', not 'issue.' Sic is short for the Latin *sic erat scriptum*, 'thus was it written'. Yes, it qualifies as another hip literary device. It's what authors or editors do when they print something verbatim that is obviously erroneous, logically dubious or just plain stupid. It's a high-class way of pointing a finger and going 'Ha ha!'

‡ Urinary output. That's where the ureter from the kidney empties into the bladder. The UO in question was not blocked (thank God), just hiding behind part of the tumour.

portable machine on a rolling stand. The wand resembles a 1960s men's electric shaver, attached to a cord that feeds back into the scanner.

But the world of ultrasound scanning is apparently not one-size-fits-all. I'm back at Kings, although this time I'm up one storey from Urology, on the second floor of the hospital's Golden Jubilee Wing. This is one of seven wings (along with the Critical Care Centre) in the main building, complementing the 26 outbuildings on campus.

It's a big place, and like many things British, it's built on an irregular plan, one thing jammed alongside the next, late twentieth century glass and steel abutting early nineteenth century brick and stone. Although the British provided the science for the U.S. Land Ordinance of 1785 (allowing the western US territories to be plotted into pleasing, logical and symmetrical grids), they never used this science for themselves. Perhaps it was too late. Maybe eight centuries of building along cart tracks and game trails will do that to your infrastructure.

As instructed, I arrived with a full bladder, having consumed the requisite half litre of water in the previous hour. By doctor's order, despite the pain of urination, I drink more than two litres per day, and am in and out of the loo more often than a Saturday night pub crawler.

The Kings ultrasound department is surprisingly small, just like the machines themselves. Same type of waiting room. No TV, no magazines, bog-standard* NHS chairs (which are surprisingly comfortable), an information stand. An institutional paint job. I gave my name to the receptionist and took a seat. 10 minutes went by, and then 20. I began tapping my foot. After a few minutes more, my pain level moved quickly from Nuisance through Trouble, heading toward Sweating. I had to whizz like yesterday. My name was finally

* Bog-standard means unexceptional or completely ordinary. 'Bog' is a slang word for toilet. There are many fun and interesting theories about where the term came from but the actual derivation is unknown.

called, and I entered a very small room with an examination bed and a nurse, who had a portable ultrasound machine on a rolling cart. It was called BladderScan, which is accurate if unimaginative. Sort of like naming your daughter Girl.

I assumed the position, which in this case was on my back with my trousers and shorts pulled down just above the pubic tubercles.* The nurse took the conveniently pre-chilled gel and spread it over my exposed and vulnerable belly. Then the probe† was wielded with professional diligence. I didn't know she would press so hard. If she had used her elbow it would have been no more uncomfortable. But that's because of the full bladder, which by this time, several weeks post-symptom onset, is now critically painful.

I moved quickly through Sweating into Wincing, which I hoped was not becoming my new normal. To the nurse's credit, she was quick, friendly and efficient. Thankfully, she offered no narration. I was finally released to use the toilet, which was rarely my happy place any more, but was then, despite the pain of it. I was also safe to travel home, because I wouldn't have to go to the loo again for another hour.

---

17 May, 2019

Another trip to Kings today, another waiting room, and another full bladder, this time for a CT scan. There was some kind of mix-up with the scheduling, and the department was

* These are the bones that lie under your abdomen, supporting the intestines, at the same height as the hip bones. In other words, she may or may not have seen something personal. These bones are not to be confused with the superior pubic rames or the ischial tuberosities. But you knew that.

† There's that action verb again.

also understaffed. I hunkered down for a long siege: foot-tapping, rocking in my chair and potential crotch-grabbing (my own) as I waited for the blessed relief of the loo when it was over. To my surprise, I was the first in line, but not for the scan suite. I was shuffled into a phlebotomist's chair, facing a man who was clearly a veteran arm-sticker. He trussed me in a tourniquet with business-like speed, and like every needle pusher in Britain, intoned the phrase, 'Sharp scratch!'

Instead of taking blood, he fitted me with a cannula, a removable tap into my circulatory system. A radioactive dye would be injected through it just before the scan. That would be the moment of truth, where I'd find out through raw experimentation whether I had an allergy to the mildly radioactive solution.* Rather than the immediate thrill of anaphylactic shock or the delayed ecstasy of hives, I only experienced what the experts referred to as a 'warm sensation', which sounds like nothing less than a description of wetting oneself. In reality it was more like inhaling a triple shot of hundred-proof whisky.

In that happy instance, the heat begins in the chest and quickly tramples through the entire body, and then one falls over. In the CT clinic, I simply got the heat. It was like the best of my old drinking days with none of the consequences. Thoroughly disappointing.

A CT scan is easy, unless you're claustrophobic, I suppose. Lie on the bed, in you go, out you come, 10 minutes tops. It was almost as fast as an automated car wash, although there were fewer visuals, and no chance of a quick make-out session with the passenger. As always, I was in a rush to use the toilet. But I had to wait, because someone was in there.

Someone.

Very.

Slow.

---

* Truthfully, I already knew this from a previous operation in March 2019. That's where we actually did the raw experimentation. See the flashback in the upcoming entry for 22 May, 2019.

I dodged wetting myself by quickly striding back and forth and doing knee bends, to the amusement of passers-by. Finally, my important business concluded, it was safe to travel home, because remember: I won't have to go to the loo again for another hour.

---

21 May, 2019

As on many Tuesday afternoons, I joined the volunteer team at the Healing Rooms of SW London. It's part of a worldwide network under the International Association of Healing Rooms, based in Spokane, Washington. There are hundreds of certified Christian Healing Rooms in 64 nations at the time of this writing.* Our group in SW London is typical. We're just a group of Christians, none of us special. What we have in common is the faith that God will heal through prayer in the name of Jesus, just as He did in the time of the Apostles.†

I revealed (not exclusively) my situation to my teammates, told them I refused to receive the diagnosis, and declared that I would be healed. This was followed by my standard declaration, now with a kicker, 'I have a strong, healthy body and a powerful immune system that rejects sickness and disease, *including cancer!*'

'Amen!' they agreed, and then laid hands on me and prayed individually for my health and healing. I wasn't divinely

---

* Information from http://healingrooms.com (accessed March 6, 2020)

† See Acts chapter 3:1-10 for one example. I realise there are many Christians who don't accept this theologically, claiming instead that miracles ceased after the time of the Apostles, that an unchanging God changed His nature, as it were. Please show me that in the Bible. My experience says otherwise.

delivered right then, but that's okay. It didn't change my thinking or knock my faith.

After all, Elijah had to pray seven times for a drought to be broken. Christ told Peter he had to forgive 'seventy times seven.' The man by the pool at Bethesda waited 38 years for his miracle. The point in every case was, *Keep asking!* So I did. And I will.

But asking isn't the end of it. I live in the world and am still subject to the world's rules. But it's complicated sometimes. Guidance from the Anglican Church says 'Prayer for healing and strengthening should not involve the rejection of the skills and activity of medicine which are also part of God's faithfulness to creation.'*

This directive about making use of physicians comes from the book of Ecclesiasticus (not Ecclesiastes), also known as the Book of Sirach. Written between 200 and 175 BC, it isn't part of the Jewish canon, but is considered divinely inspired by the Catholic Church. It contains good advice, and was a key to confidently taking my next steps.

Sirach 38:1-4 reads [1]'Honor physicians for their services, for the Lord created them; [2]for their gift of healing comes from the Most High, and they are rewarded by the king. [3]The skill of physicians makes them distinguished, and in the presence of the great they are admired. [4]The Lord created medicines out of the earth, and the sensible will not despise them.'

I consider myself a sensible person, but I also know God heals through prayer. I've witnessed it. Does that make me a hypocrite for not going for a 100% miraculous cure? Alternatively, would I be foolish to place all my hope in it? I was willing to be called a hypocrite (the Bible says I will scorned regardless), and too frightened to limit myself to prayer only. Instead, I get to walk down the middle and paraphrase Buzz Lightyear: 'To surgery --- *AND BEYONNND!*'

---

* https://www.churchofengland.org/prayer-and-worship/worship-texts-and-resources/common-worship/wholeness-and-healing/wholeness-and-healing (accessed 27 March 2020)

22 May, 2019

I now had a surgery date. Instead of D-Day (Debridement Day) being 6 June, it is 4 June, in the now-familiar confines of King's Hospital. The invasion was about to begin.

The news about the surgery came by official letter. I'm used to these letters. NHS has been my most faithful correspondent since I arrived in Britain in the summer of 2018. The reason I knew Kings so well is that I'd already been a surgical patient there. Let me take you on a quick walkabout and then we'll get back to the current story.

In late 2018 I asked my GP for guidance about an ongoing and worsening swallowing problem, or dysphagia. For about seven years I'd had trouble swallowing easily and would often cough spasmodically after eating. This was worsening steadily, and sometimes it would bring food back into my mouth. At least it wasn't Christine Taylor in Dodgeball, 'throwing up in her mouth a little bit'*- it wasn't vomit. After ruling that out, my GP referred me to Kings for examination. He didn't think it was cancer, but – remember that 'fast track' I mentioned earlier? He put it on a fast track. Just in case.

I was eventually diagnosed with a condition called *pharyngeal pouch*. This is a rare situation where part of the oesophageal wall blows out and creates a little sac. Food and drink get trapped there instead of going down into the tummy like good little boys and girls. Pharyngeal pouch is potentially

* The urban dictionary term for this is 'vurping.' There's no actual medical term for the phenomenon, which is caused by GORD, Gastro-Oesophogeal Reflux Disease, sometimes called acid reflux. Like you and every doctor aren't going to keep calling it 'vurping.'

dangerous, because material might dislodge during sleep and aspirate into my lungs, creating an infection. Or my windpipe might be spontaneously blocked altogether, leaving me to die quietly and helplessly from suffocation.

Regardless, it meant sleeping on my back was my only option. Any other position and things leaked. Pharyngeal pouch is easily corrected surgically but the doctors want to know the field of play ahead of time. So, a pre-surgical CT was done, which is where I found out I wasn't allergic to radioactive tracers.

As an unexpected bonus, I was hustled to the front of the surgical queue. I apparently had an exceptional case and my surgeon wanted the process beamed live to a teaching hospital in Manchester. I was to be a star! Fortunately, I was unconscious for the tour guide portion of *that* adventure.

The surgery turned out well, by the way. When it was over, I was pain-free, vurp free, and feeling better than ever, just in time to be given a cancer diagnosis two months later.

Back to the CT scan. The tech strapped me onto something like the rescue boards used to take the injured off mountains. This was bolted onto a motorised stand in front of the scanner. It was a slow-motion carnival ride. I was scanned vertically, then horizontally, then with my head down – all to see what the contents of the pouch did in various scenarios, for a truly 3-D picture.

The tech lured me into viewing the images on the way out, but he had an ulterior motive. 'Your pouch is big but not the most interesting I've seen,' he said matter-of-factly as I turned to leave.

'Oh? How's that?'

The expression on his face revealed (not exclusively – there was a second technician in the room) he was about to tell me something for effect.

'We had a guy in here a couple of years ago whose pouch was so big, and gave him so much trouble, he took to cleaning it out with a spoon.'

This page intentionally left blank
so you can recover from that image.

26 May, 2019

Sometimes when I concentrate on God, I get visions. It's always been like this; it's just the way I was made. On this particular day, I was given a vision of a mighty storm.

I was standing in the door of my house looking out at it. I saw lashing rain and the almost ceaseless lightning. The roaring thunder thudded in my chest and rattled the storm door. But none of it touched me.

I pushed the door closed, and bolted it against the storm. I was locked in tight. I no longer heard the rain drumming on the roof. The sound of thunder faded, and the lightning flashes were blocked by the shutters.

Turning from the door, I set another log on the fire, which was already burning merrily. My home was tight, warm, dry and strong, and built on a solid foundation.

The vision was a reassurance, the first of many, that everything was going to turn out all right. I needed every one of those that I received in the weeks to come. Because there were many days where I wasn't so sure.

---

28 May, 2019

Before I was allowed on the operating table, an assessment was made to ensure I was healthy enough to handle the TURBT. Blood test, BP, resting pulse, oxygen saturation: the usual. The nurse exclusively revealed that I'm as healthy as can be. A doctor then ran through the procedure, which is relatively straightforward. A rigid device (with attached light and camera) called a resectoscope is the star of the show. It's a Swiss Army Knife version of the cystoscope.

With it, the surgeon will carve away at the tumour like its a shawarma, until there's a danger of cutting through the bladder wall. Bladder perforation is very dicey, as you can imagine, and I'd lay odds that any surgeon responsible for that would say a bad word, possibly two. The bladder is almost impossible to repair surgically and a gross mistake like that would have made my recovery (and the rest of my life) very different than it was.

I'd wake up after surgery with a catheter and a bag, he said. I get to take these home for a couple of days. I'm instructed on how to use it and care for it, and how to deal with it during the night. I don't know about you, but my strong opinion is that urine should go directly in the toilet and not be stored for later. Not that I'll have a choice.

---

3 June, 2019

Before we head into surgery, let's scrub. I have some dirt to wash off.

I have to believe there's a strong connection between our spiritual and emotional natures, as well as the things that happen in our bodies. For a simple example, picture a sad person stooped over, as though carrying a physical burden.

Much research has been done on this mind-body connection. A 30 year-study with more than one million participants found a strong link between stress-related disorders, or PTSD, and auto-immune diseases.* Those are conditions where the body

---

* https://jamanetwork.com/journals/jama/article-abstract/2685155

attacks itself like Celiac Disease, Rheumatoid Arthritis, Type 1 Diabetes or Multiple Sclerosis.

Obviously then, people who have been beaten up by life sometimes then begin beating up on their own bodies. I think there's a spiritual aspect to this.

Okay – let's come to a full stop right here. This is all my opinion, and there's no medical or (to my knowledge) scriptural basis for what I believe.* That's okay – you may believe that the Detroit Tigers will win the World Series sometime in the next decade. That's no less crazy-sounding to my way of thinking.

Any family physician will agree that life conditions can cause body changes. Stress from poverty, physical or emotional fatigue, grief, unexpected crises: any or all of these can lead to high blood pressure, insomnia, indigestion and the like.

In the same way, it makes sense to me that my attitudes and the words I use to express those attitudes could, over time, influence my body. There are also expressions that reflect seemingly-related bodily conditions. A stubborn person is said to have a stiff neck. A clumsy person has two left feet.

I spent many many years of my life in a deep unhappiness. There were vast numbers of circumstances that I found *hard to swallow*. The manifestation of this in a pharyngeal pouch makes sense to me as my body's response to a spiritual sickness. Now, this bladder cancer diagnosis.

For about 35 years, my general attitude about life was very sarcastic and cynical. How I felt about many things was easily summed up in the phrase (pardon my language), *'Piss on it!'* I carried a lot of anger and bitterness for a long, long time. Being sexually abused and bullied as a child can do that. That's the story of my first book (shamelessly plugged here for the last time).

As has been shown in peer-reviewed research, trauma can trigger the body to attack itself, and few things provide a more obscene or vicious attack than cancer.

---

* If you happen to know any such scriptural references, I would be grateful to hear about them. Just email editor@alansearle.media.

Because of all this, I'm completely unsurprised that if I were to develop a tumour, it would be in my bladder. Even if there's no link that can be proven, and no one to agree with me that there's a spiritual connection between these things, the irony alone is too much to pass up.

Yes, these are the things I ponder in the middle of the night, even when I'm slated for surgery the next day.

---

4 June, 2019

I began the day with a 7:00 a.m. prayer meeting. The man I was paired with was a physician. When we were done with our church business, Michael prayed for me, for my surgeon and the surgical team. It was the first of many health-related prayers to come. My surgery was scheduled for 12:30, and I arrived early, as instructed, with an empty stomach. Being handed the requisite backless gown, I was shown into a small ward with several beds and accompanying hanging screens.

I pulled mine closed long enough to disrobe and don what passes for an NHS fashion statement, then re-opened the screen, awaiting further direction. There was a second man across the small room, doing the same. As he verified his identity by reciting his name and birthdate, I discovered that we had the same name with the same spelling and the same birthday. It was a bizarre coincidence.

When it was my turn, I verified my identity, earning a delightfully cute NHS Urologic Surgery Collectible Series wrist band. I answered a few questions about my condition: '*Yes, I fasted. Yes, I feel good. Yes, I have someone coming for me after the surgery. No, I'm not allergic to any medication*'. I did so well at this I was allowed to lie down on the bed and then given a wild ride, immediately and without warning. I was wheeled off into the vastness of Kings College Hospital.

Seriously, Kings is large enough that I'm certain it takes new employees a week just to find the loo. This would be important because there are no fewer than seven Costa Coffee locations on campus. This was torture to me as a java-loving urology patient. I smelt coffee everywhere, but was denied it by doctor's order.

When I arrived at the surgical suite after what felt like a high-speed police chase, I again verified my identity and answered all the same questions as before. I was then fitted with another cannula. This one was inserted into a vein on the back of my left arm, just above the wrist.

The surgeon popped in and introduced himself, exuding teeth and confidence. He would be the one driving the resectoscope to cut the tumour. It's described as a routine procedure and easy to do by remote. That's because clean saline solution is swished in and out of the bladder during the procedure, to make sure he can see past the bleeding.*

A few moments later, the anaesthesiologist floated in to say hi, as mellow as any stoned hippie chick in the movie Woodstock. I cast about vainly for a whiff of patchouli oil. She asked me for the third time if I'm allergic to anything, specifically propofol. I assured her I am not. I'm reminded the propofol will cause me to be light-headed and mentally slow when I come to. The assembly line went pretty fast. Away we went.

The last thing I saw before going under was teeth and confidence. The first thing I saw upon waking was Angel #3. She was standing by with a syringe plugged into my cannula. Her gentle voice floated into my consciousness before my eyes came into focus. 'How you feelin' lovely?' she asked.

---

* https://medigence.com/treatment/trans-urethral-resection-of-bladder-tumor

As was promised, I felt dizzy and light-headed from the propofol, and struggled for an appropriate answer to that question, as well as one *can* think after being voluntarily unconscious. I vaguely remembered Doctor Patcholi reminding me that the propofol would not address post-surgical pain. This explained the rapidly spreading burning sensation in my groin.

'Hurts,' I grunted. I was now reduced to one word responses, half of what I managed during my star turn on *Strictly Come Cystoscopy* a few weeks prior. My brevity was not from pain this time, but from the relentless anaesthetic hangover.

'I'll take care of that,' she said, smiling sweetly. Morphine, you never tasted so good. Angel #3, you are now my new best friend. After about 45 minutes of pain management and vital sign monitoring, I was signed out in the care of my wife, and wheeled with great ceremony (or so it appeared to my opiate-addled brain) to the car park.*

Somehow at home I managed to pull myself successfully up all 30 stairs to our second floor flat, catheter, bag and all, whereupon I collapsed gratefully into my bed. I was now in the urine storage business. What a hassle.

---

5 June, 2019

Sometime after midnight I came awake, lying on my back. I'm used to this, staring at the ceiling in the dark, after so many years of living with the pharyngeal pouch. I should get up and

* I was reminded by the inestimable Mrs. Searle during the editing of this book that I actually *walked* (shuffled slowly) to the car, I did *not* ride in a chair. Morphine must have worked better than I originally thought. Also, for the record, please note that 'inestimable' is another five-syllable word.

go to the toilet, I thought, because that's the normal thing to do. Then I remembered. The catheter. The bag.

I lay there with an aquarium tube running from my penis to a super-sized night-time catheter bag. This was slumped over sadly in a household bucket next to the bed. I squeezed the bag; it was as rigid as a freshly-baked haggis. That explained my urgency: I was experiencing the urological equivalent of the A4 through Hammersmith during Friday afternoon rush hour. A total backup. 'Queues May Form'.

I managed to sit up without catching the tube and shuffled off to the toilet, hauling the bucket. I lifted out the distended bag and fumbled with the spout, which had a stopcock identical to the one on my two litre hydration backpack. There's food for thought, but not now. I opened the spout and let 'er rip. It's the closest I'd had to a truly satisfying whizz in many weeks. Finished, I drank another 300 ml of water (as prescribed) and carefully made my way back to bed.

I slept through the rest of the night for the first time in I don't know how long. In the morning, Melanie was off to work and I had the day to myself. Just me and my catheter and my bag and my paracetamol. I somehow managed to park myself on the sofa and binge-watch Star Trek: Deep Space Nine without falling asleep.

Probably because I'm a farm kid (idle hands are the devil's playground, you know), I dislike 'doing nothing'. However, I had no energy to slice or fry my inner couch potato. I began wondering about the catheter though, and decided to satisfy my curiosity. I was carrying what's called a Foley catheter, designed by Dr. Frederic Foley in 1929. It's held in place by a small balloon at the tip, which is inflated once it's properly inserted into the bladder. Yes, its possible to improperly insert a catheter. More about that later.

The word catheter comes from the Greek *kathiénai*, which means 'to thrust into.'* Gee, thanks for that. The earliest recorded use of catheters was by the Egyptians in about 1,500 BC. These were metal tubes, reeds or even curled up palm leaves. Hippocrates mentioned them. One was found in the rubble of Pompeii (how did archaeologists know what it was?)

Amazingly, there is such a thing as 'intermittent self-catheterization', in which the user inserts and removes the catheter as needed. Apparently some people can handle doing this. Not I. I would quickly run out of slide-whistle sound effects for that.

Even more exciting, catheters can be customised! Yes, just like your new car, there are various designs and packages available for the discriminating new catheter buyer. One medical supply company (which shall remain nameless) offers no fewer than 11 bag designs, depending on whether you are jogging, enjoying a night at the opera, or at home in pain, binge-watching Star Trek: Deep Space Nine.

These companies are just like auto dealerships. They have their own parts departments. Yes, if you don't want to drive your catheter and bag into the service bay, you can throw it onto the workbench in your garage and have at it yourself. Unlike cystoscopes, used urinary catheters are not available on eBay. There is a wide range of new catheter accessories though, but I have yet to locate any in designer colours.

---

* These delightful facts about the catheter are from the United States National Institutes of Health. https://www.ncbi.nlm.nih.gov/pmc/articles/PMC4673556/ (accessed 12 Mar. 2020). The authors of the article say an alternative to the Foley Catheter is badly needed, claiming it costs NHS 'between £1.0–2.5 billion (annually) and accounts for 2100 deaths per year.'

6 June, 2019

I get my catheter pulled today. The medical term is probably 'removed,' but why stop being graphic now? For this procedure I shuffled myself back to Kings College Hospital. After assuring Melanie that I would be Just Fine and Would Manage, she agreed that I could go alone. The Urology Unit had said walk in any time. Or shuffle in, as it was.

The reason for the shuffling had less to do with the bag strapped to my left leg, and more to do with the tube running into it. More specifically, the tube running out of me. Even more specifically, the point at which the tube is running out of me.* It was MyTube, as opposed to YouTube.

The wretched thing irritated me when I walked, even after some additional strapping-things-down to keep random flapping to a minimum. Hence, I shuffled meekly to the bus stop instead of striding boldly. My fellow passengers were very gracious. They all stayed out of my way, gave me plenty of room, let me board first, and offered me a prime seat. They acted like I was old and infirm, WHICH I AM NOT. I merely had a temporary addendum to my water works.

Back in the Urology Unit, nothing had changed. Same dull waiting room. Same rows of pensioners (I'm clearly the youngest in the room at age 62). Same lack of reading material. Even Angel #2 was there. I avoided her malevolent gaze by hiding behind my newspaper and prayed desperately for Angel #1. Being catheterised, I felt secretly superior to the other patients. 'Ha! I can wait out the lot of you. You can all go *twice* before I do, for all I care!' I've become used to taking my small victories where I may, petty though they are.

* My experience with urologists is that despite many years of medical school in a field having to do with, among other things, the penis, they somehow cannot bring themselves to say the word 'penis.' Their universally preferred term is 'water works.'

My prayer was answered, Angel #2 suddenly looked at her watch and left, presumably on break. Angel #1 appeared in her stead, and walked me back into an examination room. On the way, she asked if I wanted a chaperone. NHS wisely and humanely offers chaperones for any situation or procedure one may deem overly personal. I knew I faced months of people viewing and handling my nether regions so, what the hey. Water Works is no longer just a card in Monopoly.

'All right, then pull down your trousers and lie back on the bed,' she said.

Because it was Angel #1 and not Angel #2 I complied, knowing I would never bother to count how many female plumbers would handle my water works through all this. Angel deflated the balloon and I queued up my mental slide whistle. How pleasurable to have a large foreign object removed from a most sensitive orifice! I felt like a million bucks while I shuffled home. I was physically able to walk boldly, but shuffling *does* lead to the best seat on the bus.

---

8 June, 2019

Four days after surgery I was hardy enough to attend an all-afternoon social event. The pain was subsiding although the haematuria continued. But the bleeding was now less threatening than before surgery. Now there was a good *reason* that blood and clots appeared when I stood over the commode. It was now somehow reasonable, because it was a sign of healing.

This may sound odd, especially if you carry shame around bodily functions, but every time I unzipped, I thanked the Lord for healing me. We'd probably all be amazed at how many prayers are issued worldwide from people in toilets.

---

19 June, 2019

Life continued as it does. Dental appointment. Volunteer sessions at the Healing Rooms. Driving lessons. A driving exam. Yes, I had to take a road test. About six weeks after arriving in London in August 2018, my wallet disappeared. It fell out of my pocket, was pinched, lost, something.[*]

It forced my hand about getting a UK driving license since my American license was no more. Being a farm boy who's used to driving almost anything, I was more than willing to take my test. But prudence[†] prevailed and I took some driving lessons. This turned out to be a good idea, because if you want to legally drive a standard transmission in the UK you have to drive one during the test. I don't own one, but the driving schools do.

Taking lessons actually was important because there's a particular etiquette to driving in London. Mastering it makes motoring less like dodge-em karts on a primary school playground and more like slow-motion ballet. I found there's a certain grace to it, once I got acclimatised.

Amusingly, although I've been driving since age 12, I failed my first exam in spectacular and dramatic fashion. For the last manoeuvre on the test, we were moving through a large multi-lane roundabout in a 30 mph zone.[‡] The examiner managed to hit the brakes just in time to prevent us from being fatally

---

* I may as well plug my website as well as my book. I wrote up the wallet incident at this link: https://alansearle.media/2020/04/23/anxiety-or-rest/

† Actually, my wife's name is Melanie, not Prudence. She's Formula One qualified, so I never *ever* argue with her about driving.

‡ Yet another thing I love about the UK. Although many measurements are always expressed metrically, perhaps due to Britain's long uneasy marriage to the EU, road distances are still in miles and yards (!) and speeds remain in miles per hour.

crushed by a lorry the size of the HMS Queen Elizabeth. Used to driving on the right, I was, of course, looking the wrong way.

---

20 June, 2019

My bleeding had become periodic and then stopped altogether after a couple of weeks. I should have been happy, but I was frustrated instead. After throat surgery in April, I'd bounced back fast, in mere days. Was that really only three months ago? I'd felt so good in early April. Now I was tired, and weak, and continued to be in pain.

The fortnight since the surgery had also been one for deep reflection. You might recall that I mentioned 10 or 15 entries ago that I refused to let this diagnosis redefine me in any way? But now the rub came. How I felt was vastly different from what I believed to be true.

Remember what I wrote? *I say what I believe and I believe what I say*. How I perceive things always influences how I speak of them. How I speak of them influences what I believe about them. Finally, what I believe about them strengthens my faith. Or not. It's a simple formula, but some days it was a very long journey from point A to point B.

My mindset can work for me or against me. The book of Romans has a very important instruction about this. It says that if I focus on my physical circumstances, I end up on a death march. If I think about spiritual things, I obtain both life and peace.*

* 'To be carnally minded is death, but to be spiritually minded is life and peace' - Romans 8:6.

'In fact, the mindset focused on the flesh fights God's plan and refuses to submit to his direction, because it cannot!'* So, as My Personal Health Care Journey proceeded, the time came for me to concentrate on the promises God made to me about my life. None of them mentioned dying of cancer. Cancer had to remain a lie.

---

* Romans 8:7 (TPT)

PART TWO:

TRIAL

21 June, 2019

I was referred by the specialists at Kings for treatment at Guy's Hospital. This began with a new game: Meet the Oncologists. Guy's has one of the world's foremost cancer treatment facilities, and this day we were sitting in Guy's Urology Centre. Same deal as Kings, bigger waiting room.* The first stop after providing the obligatory blood and urine samples was with a surgeon, Dr. Fervoro. Melanie and I were surprised to be with a surgeon. Wasn't this meeting about oncology? Y'know, chemo and losing your hair and stuff?

Dr. Fervoro was brisk, businesslike and enthusiastic. He dove into a detailed description of surgical bladder removal and scribbled circles and ovals and lines on a blank piece of paper. There are several related procedures, the names of which reflect their complexity. There's the cystectomy, the radical cystectomy, the cystoprostatectomy and the cysto-prostato-urethrectomy.†

What you get (or lose, as it were) depends on what he scoops out, which depends further on what he finds. The best part? We may not know beforehand what it will look like afterwards. Need higher blood pressure? Try that right there.

In all cases, he gleefully explained, my insides would be vastly re-plumbed. He outlined how I might wake up with my urine draining into a bag via a hole in my abdomen. He excitedly described how he might take part of my intestine to fashion a bladder substitute that would drain through the penis. The idea

* I'm exceedingly grateful to everyone I encountered at King's College Hospital on the first part of my journey. You are kind, dedicated professionals who know your business and care for your patients. I was well tended and love you all. Even you, Angel #2. But only because Jesus says I have to.

† At 10 syllables, it's the longest word in this book.

of a fake bladder draining through the God-given water works was supposed to give me a reassurance of normalcy.

Sadly, though, such work-arounds can leak because man-made bladder substitutes have no muscle control. Welcome to the world of voluntary catheterisation.*

Another plan would have part of the intestine made into a reservoir, which is drained manually by a catheter inserted into part of the intestine that sticks out of the abdomen. My insides would be outside. Freaky. I was shocked at the idea that there was no certainty what things would look like when I came to, begging for morphine. The options were all *his* options, not my options.

As he droned on, I tuned out. I'd had enough. It was bad, wondering what it would be like to have a penis less useful than a four-fingered glove. So, I drifted into a fantasy, musing on why there was no better answer for this. There were plenty of devices for urine cachement *outside* the body, why not inside? Pig heart valves have been transplanted into humans for years, why not baboon bladders?

I returned to reality just as Dr. Fervoro finished dizzily sketching and explaining. I was completely fazed, and a bit woozy at all of his undesirable outcomes, and was ready to zoom out of there into the nearest pub.† It was clear the man knew his trade. He thrived on the challenge of saving lives by cutting people open and reworking in his image what God had created in His.

This isn't to denigrate him or his talent or his knowledge. I'm grateful for all that. He saves lives, after all. It just freaks me out that someone was eager to do that for a living. It was a 15 minute discussion more unsettling than an hour of shock

* I forgot to mention earlier that the NHS catheter instruction booklet gives advice on how to have sex while wearing a catheter. I skipped that section. I didn't want to know. Just, no.

† You'll find five zeds in short order there. Just to make up for their absence elsewhere. Very stylised, no?

therapy. I didn't like the sound of any of it. Melanie and I staggered back into the waiting room, only to be called again.

[What Dr. Fervoro's drawing looked like. I continue to kick myself for discarding the original. It was much more intimidating. He actually broke a pencil tip and ripped little cuts in the paper from pushing so hard.]

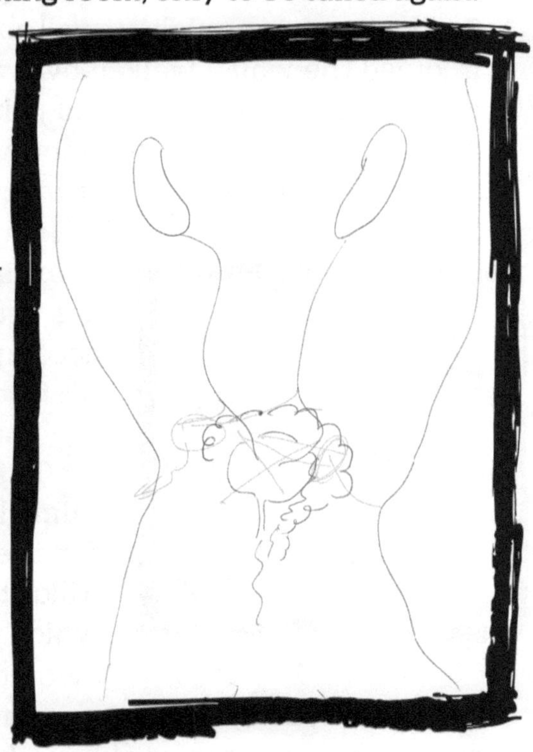

The Urology Centre waiting room is often packed on clinic days, and today was no exception. I was very agitated at what we'd just heard, and wanted to walk it off. However, there was no more room to walk than to sit, so I stood. I issued a silent selfish prayer that whatever else happened on this journey, it wouldn't lead to surgery.

With rare exceptions, bladder cancer cases at Guy's begin with chemotherapy and then move either to radiotherapy, or surgery. Unless, that is, the patient goes AWOL and refuses further treatment. That's my right under law, but I had nowhere near enough faith to refuse treatment and put myself 100% in God's hands for a cure. After all, medicine exists for a reason, right?

After barely escaping alive from The Revelation of Doctor Fervero, I stood in semi-shock pondering what was next. Suddenly, my eye caught a small object on the floor, right where it joined the wall. I walked over and bent down for a closer look. It was a spring from a ball-point pen. 'That's odd,' I thought as I picked it up. Who finds a spring at random like that?

An inner voice said, 'You will spring to new life'.

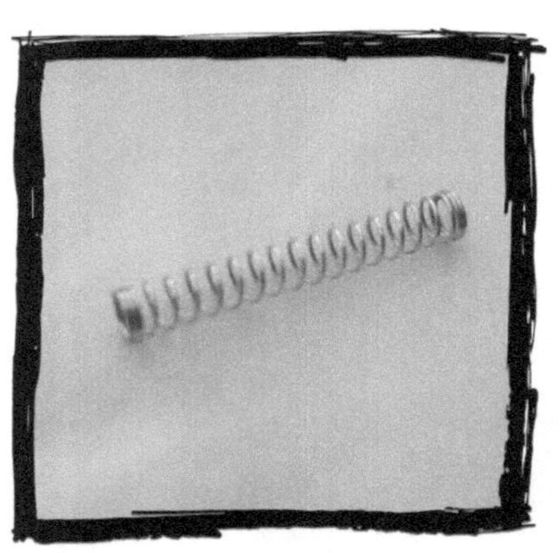

I should explain. When God wants me to know something, it's usually with an 'inner voice' accompanied by a *certainty* that it's from the Lord.

'You will spring to new life'.

This was a reassurance. It calmed me down and prepared me for the next meeting, where Dr. Milda told us about chemotherapy, which would begin for me in July. I would sit through three 21-day cycles, with drug infusions on days one and eight. It did not sound like the Summer of Love. Instead, if Dr. Milda's telling was correct, it might be the Summer of Puking. She assured me that I'd be ill. Big time.

---

22 June, 2019

I awoke the next morning aware that although life was about to become very different, life would go on. I lay in half sleep, reviewing the hospital visit of the day before and what I thought was a specific message from God.

'You will spring to new life.' What was I supposed to make of that?

Have faith, I concluded. I'm not alone in this. Surrender, remember? Ask for prayer, as much as I can get. Continue to declare that I have a strong, healthy body and a powerful immune system that rejects sickness and disease, *including cancer.* Take full advantage of the free medical treatment I'm being offered. Don't lose heart.

Meanwhile, life was to go on, which on this particular day meant installing new linoleum in the kitchen. This required moving appliances so I could place flooring underneath them. When I moved the washing machine, I found another spring. There was no clue where it may have come from. To find a spring at random is strange enough. Two in two days? I'll take that as confirmation of God's message for me.

'You will spring to new life.'

I was about to undergo a trial, a trial that had to do with cancer, and also things beyond cancer. When all was said and done, I would spring to new life. God said so, and I had to take Him at His word.

What I didn't realise then was that I'd started down a slippery slope the day before, and had placed myself in danger. What I described as 'my selfish prayer' about avoiding surgery wasn't actually a prayer. There are prayers, and then there are prayers, remember? No, it had been a demand, and it would eventually lead to big trouble.

---

23 June, 2019

It's Sunday. We're at church. I was again reminded of God's goodness and His promises as the Rev. Jamie Mulvaney preached. 'In the name of Jesus,' he said, 'we have victory over all things, and power over all things. We cast aside the ever-changing narrative of the world in favour of the never-changing narrative of Jesus Christ.'

I won't build a case for that here, because it's not fair to drag you past Theology 101. Suffice it to say I believed Jamie, and was about to put it to trial. In the coming months, my ability to ignore the world around me in favour of the world inside me *would* be a test. It was a pass-fail test. God doesn't grade on a curve.

Everyone who's on trial must have a good defence. Melanie and I began fashioning ours by building what we called our Wall of Declarations. We took God's truths and wrote them out on sticky notes and posted them, so we would constantly be reminded of them.

They said things like:

- Death and life are in the power of the tongue
- Other people's words about cancer don't affect me
- My faith rests in the power of God, not in human wisdom
- Fear, you are not my master
- Cancer, you are not my master
- Jesus is my master

---

24 June, 2019

With our defence plotted, we now needed expert witnesses. Melanie reached out to a half-dozen friends who became our Faithful Pray-ers. We started with the truths outlined above, and asked our friends to stand in agreement with them. Here was our prayer for Week One: *'In the name of Jesus Christ we command all cancer cells to leave Alan's body. We speak life and health to his immune system to rise up and destroy all cancer in Jesus' name. Cancer, you are not our master. Jesus is our master.'*

One partner responded to me directly with words from Psalm 27, '*"I believe I will see the goodness of the Lord in the land of the living." So Alan, "Wait on the Lord; be strong, and may your heart be stout; wait on the Lord."*' Good advice. Waiting equals surrender. My brain had been working overtime ever since watching Dr Fervoro imitate Bob Ross. Why did these doctors have to narrate everything? As a long-time radio presenter I can only say that I have small tolerance for amateurs.

During my orientation for chemotherapy the previous week, I was handed several pages of information, including a list of possible side effects and how to respond to them. I engaged in what I call 'prophetic editing', putting a bold line through each symptom, and writing NO! I refused to agree with any of what was 'expected'. I declared that I'd suffer none of it. It was all a bunch of lies, I said to myself, just like the cancer itself.

If I believe Christ overcame all things, then I should move ahead with an attitude of victory. Victory over all the side-effects that I was told are 'expected.' Victory over my own bad attitudes. Victory over the amount of time this would take out of my life. Victory over the plans I had to cancel. Victory over any fear. Victory over pride.

Victory over cancer.

1 July 2019

More pictures today, this time from an MRI, both pelvic and thoracic, so they can see the kidneys as well as the bladder. These will complement the pre-surgical CT scan as visual references for the starting line in this race. The MRI also provided the best possible news, which was an answer to many, many prayers by many, many people. The tumour was indeed a stage 2 tumour, not stage 3, meaning it hadn't grown past the bladder muscle, making treatment easier.

In the UK treatment scheme, chemotherapy is followed by radiotherapy IF the tumour responds well enough to the chemo. If not, its back to the surgical suite, although the patient has some input.* Things were looking up. Thanks to having that 'strong healthy body and a powerful immune system that rejects sickness and disease, *including cancer*,' I was a prime candidate for chemotherapy. Or, as Doctor Milda put it in the official report:

On examination, he looked well. His performance status is 0. His height is 190 cm and his weight 83 kg. His cardiovascular and respiratory examinations are unremarkable. His abdomen is soft and non-tender. He reports no further haematuria following TURBT. (We) will proceed with gemcitabine-cisplatin chemotherapy. We will restage him after two cycles to assess response and he is likely to proceed with the definitive treatment following his third cycle of chemotherapy.

Yes, but that 'definitive treatment' – what was it to be? Radiotherapy? Or plumbing? Here's what I was selfishly praying

* https://www.cancer.org/cancer/bladder-cancer/treating/by-stage.html

for: I did *not* <u>not</u> ***not*** want surgery. And the more I insisted on it, the more trouble I created for myself, and the more unsettled I became. God was saying 'Trust Me', but I wasn't listening.

---

4 July, 2019

It's possible to take some really strange trips through the Bible. As I read it, verses will jump out at me and themes will develop. These themes often complement the dreams or visions that I have during a particular time of my life. The dreams are sometimes encouraging, sometimes a confrontation.

I'd been getting plenty of encouragement in the previous months, but now, the tables had turned. As June became July, and chemotherapy loomed, God warned me to leave cancer treatment to Him. Instead of whining about the possibility of surgery, I should simply be praying for mercy. God was telling me I was paying attention to the wrong things. He was showing me there were parts of my life – hidden parts – where evil lurked. Perhaps there was a spiritual aspect to this diagnosis after all. Perhaps I needed a deep cleaning.

God showed me my 'Piss on it' attitude was like a dandelion. Snapping the flower or leaves off a dandelion won't kill it, even if you cut it at the ground. It will grow right back, thanks to a strong and powerful tap root. It takes deep and persistent digging to pry it all the way out. With sin, as with a weed, that's the only way to kill the thing once and for all.

The Christian life is very simple in its approach (God good, devil bad) and difficult in its execution (pursue righteousness – a right standing with God - and shun evil). Galatians 5:19-21 gives a wonderfully X-rated list of the latter: 'Adultery, sexual immorality, impurity, lewdness, idolatry, sorcery, hatred, strife, jealousy, rage, selfishness, dissensions, heresies, envy, murders, drunkenness, carousing and the like.' Sounds like a round-up of my days at University.

Fortunately, I'm not like that any more, but that doesn't make the approach or the execution any easier. In some ways my life is more difficult, if only because my choices are more momentous, and they matter more to me.

With treatment about to begin, carrying with it predictions of physical torture (as opposed to the yet-non-arriving miraculous delivery from cancer), my faith-fear fork in the road came down to this question: Had He truly said, 'You will spring to new life'?

I wanted to believe it, but doubt was a hungry dog. If God really said that, it meant, 'Stick with Me, and I'll stick with you. I can't promise it will be fun, but you'll come out the other side stronger and better.' If He didn't promise new life, and I was fooling myself, I'd be up against it soon enough. Should I trust God or the doctors? My favourite killjoy, the prophet Jeremiah, warns that if I trust in man, I'm cursed. Worse, if I turn away from God, I'll live in a lonely and (spiritually) dry place. By comparison, if my hope *is the Lord* I'll be blessed.*

Fortunately, these two things are not mutually exclusive. My *main* trust is God, because He's where the truth hangs out. But I'll also listen to the doctors, because they have the facts. As with all things in the Christian life, this is a balancing act. God says 'Do not fear!' and that's a command. But sometimes its hard to do what He says. Today was one of those days. Today, I was definitely afraid of what was to come. So, God offered still more encouragement.

---

* This is Jeremiah 17:5-7 in full (NLT): 'This is what the Lord says: Cursed are those who put their trust in mere humans, who rely on human strength and turn their hearts away from the Lord. They are like stunted shrubs in the desert, with no hope for the future. They will live in the barren wilderness, in an uninhabited salty land. But blessed are those who trust in the Lord and have made the Lord their hope and confidence.'

5 July, 2019

I was on the bus to Brixton, the 322, not a bus I normally take. The 322 is a low-ridership local route, served by a regular-sized bus, not one of London's iconic red double-deckers. It has two seats immediately behind the driver that face into the aisle. I took the first one, which gave an excellent view of the boarding door. Hanging loosely from the bottom of the door... was a spring. It hung where only I saw it. I again remembered the Lord's promise.

'You will spring to new life'.

This was startling to me. Another spring? Two of them back-to-back was strange enough. Now, a third one, within a fortnight. I began meditating on this as the bus bumped along Railton Road toward Brixton Station. Springs in the desert, watering the dry places. I remembered Jeremiah again, and how those who turn away from the Lord end up in a spiritual desert. If I'm in a desert, I need an oasis. And oases are formed by springs. Didn't Isaiah also write about this?

6 July, 2019 (Morning)

I was up early this morning, at first light, and was led in my daily study to chapter 35 of Isaiah. 'Springs will gush forth in the wilderness, and streams will water the wasteland. The parched ground will become a pool, and springs of water will satisfy the thirsty land.' That's Isaiah 35, verses six and seven in the New Living Translation. This reading was like the encouragement a coach offers to a weary runner.

Verses three and four say 'Strengthen the weak hands, and support the feeble knees. Say to those who are of a fearful heart, "Be strong, fear not. Your God will come with vengeance, even God with a recompense; He will come and save you."'

Studying through Isaiah 35 that morning picked at my memory. When I was a student at Bethel School of Supernatural Ministry (BSSM) in Redding, California two years before, I'd been given a prophetic word. It was an image of me being anointed with healing oil. I dug through my notebooks until I found the card I'd received that day. The verse accompanying the picture was that same verse four: 'Say to those who are of a fearful heart, "Be strong, fear not. Your God will come with vengeance, even God with a recompense; He will come and save you."'

Shaken, I closed my Bible and then picked up my copy of My Utmost For His Highest, by Oswald Chambers, a day-by-day devotional. My reading for the day was, amazingly, based on a portion of Isaiah 35, verse seven: 'The parched ground shall become a pool...' I was now in shock. According to the King James Bible Dictionary, there are 31,102 verses in the Bible. The juxtaposition of all these verses over and over was beyond coincidence. It shouted, *'Pay attention!'* *

Chambers talked about my fork in the road. He taught me it was not faith versus fear. It was faith versus doubt. He

---

* Isaiah 35 became my watchword during treatment. You'll find a more detailed examination of it later.

said if I listen to God, my life can be fulfilled. If I let the devil talk me out of believing God's promise could come true, it can be snatched away. Satan already had me asking whether God really *was* speaking to me. I was bouncing in and out of seriously doubting it. My question of doubt was the same age-old question the devil asked Eve before she succumbed to temptation and ate the apple: 'Did God really say..?'*

Chambers' further (and more painful) point was that God has to spend time *shaping me* before I can conform to His vision for my life, instead of my own vision. He does this until He can trust me to carry His vision on my own. Chambers' words underscored what I had come to understand, that God was about to do some spiritual treatment along with my physical treatment.

If God's vision was truly 'You will spring to new life,' as I wanted to believe, then I had nothing to fear, not even life-altering surgery. Everything in me said it was real. But doubt would creep in with fear-laden questions. What was the shaping going to look like? Was it a passable test? Remember how I said it's possible to take strange trips through the Bible? Sometimes, it turns out, the Bible takes strange trips through me.

---

6 July, 2019 (Afternoon)

My head was still buzzing from all this as Melanie and I loaded the car after breakfast for a final day trip before treatment was to begin. To the beach! It was a beautiful warm sunny day at Camber Sands, and we were having a wonderful time until her engagement ring disappeared. She had removed her rings to apply sun cream and had put them gently between her lips.

* Genesis 3:1

When she went to put them back on, the engagement band, which sits inside the split wedding band, was missing. It had somehow slipped out.

Time stopped. We froze. We prayed. Melanie searched unsuccessfully in the sand at her feet, right below where she'd been. But it wasn't there. Our effort wasn't working. Instead, it was the prayer that worked. God reminded Melanie of something by giving her a mental picture of our backpack. She had turned to it to put the cream away before reaching for the rings in her mouth. She lifted the pack off the sand and there was the ring, underneath it. 'Say to those who are of a fearful heart, "Be strong, fear not. Your God will come with vengeance, even God with a recompense; He will come and save you."'

---

9 July, 2019

It was my first day of chemotherapy at Guy's Cancer-Free Centre. That's my name for it, anyway. I didn't go there to *get* cancer, after all. I went there to get free. Besides, it's not my cancer anyway. I refused to receive the diagnosis, and instead, decided to give it to Guy. It's not my cancer, it's Guy's Cancer!

The Cancer-Free Centre is an easy commute for me, just a few stops down the Southern line. That first day, I left the train at London Bridge Station, crossed St. Thomas Street and ambled down Great Maze Pond, one of about 4,000 patients to cycle through the cutting-edge facility on a daily basis.

The Cancer-Free Centre is a lovely triangular building with wraparound glass from floor to ceiling, full of 'Villages'. I entered through the Welcome Village and then rode the lift to what's called the Chemotherapy Village. The lift doors on

C opened to (exclusively) reveal a check-in desk with a small queue. I eagerly divulged my particulars in exchange for another NHS collectible plastic wrist band.

I marked time by peering through the sliding glass doors that opened out to a balcony, and then stepped out. The balcony wraps around two sides of the building, offering spectacular views of central and south London, and the chalk downs of Kent beyond, all through a protective no-jumping screen. A nurse summoned me into a pleasant wardroom divided by a low wall, which promoted the sense of a larger rectangular space. The longer walls of the suites each sported three massive recliners. There was a floor-to-ceiling window at one end, a nurses' station at the other. I was invited to take any seat.

The recliners had motorized controls for the back and footrest, and a heating unit. Next to each was a wheeled stand from which would hang my bags of medication. My vitals were taken and I was fitted with yet another cannula on my left forearm, just above the wrist. I have thick rope-like veins that stand well out from my hands and arms: I'm a phlebotomist's dream.

Next, I ingested anti-nausea pills (Ondansetron and Aprepitant) and a diuretic. The latter, and a saline drip, were to put a little pep in my step, because I had to pass at least a half-litre before they would expose me to the chemotherapy drugs. I was now chained to the rolling stand by the cannula tube and where I went, it went. It followed me around like a hat rack. I named it Lurch, after the butler in The Addams Family. Tall, slender, not talkative. Lurch became a very intimate friend as soon as we made the first of many, many trips to the loo together. I could hide nothing from him. At least he didn't judge, and remained discreet, as a good butler should.

To measure the activity from my water works, I was handed a recyclable bowl stamped out of what appeared to be waste paper and spit. It looked remarkably like a pork pie hat. Apparently everyone thinks so, because when I referred to it as a hat and jokingly put it on my head, no one at the nurses station thought *that* was a thigh slapper. The hat had semi-readable gradations on the inside wall: 100 ml, 200 ml, up to the remarkably robust 500 ml.* When I totalled the last mark it was go time (no pun intended), and I was ready for treatment.

The first chemotherapy drug, Gemcitabine, took about a half-hour to run into my system. I watched it, listening to the little pump around Lurch's waist. Tik, tik, tik; drip, drip, drip. Next, I was stepped into a four hour infusion of a drug called Cisplatin. I watched it too. Tik, tik, tik; drip, drip, drip. Lurch and I were up about every half-hour for drainage. He had a battery pack, so I unplugged him from the wall, loosely looped the power cord, and hung it off one of his hooks. That first day I accidentally wrapped the cannula tube around Lurch's body and it stopped the drip. Lurch didn't like this and began beeping furiously. He beeped again later when the bag ran out.

After five hours in (and out of) the recliner, Lurch's alert signalled the end of the Cisplatin, which was followed by a full litre of saline flush. Another hour. More mileage in and out of the toilet. I got my 10,000 steps in. This is called Gem-Cis therapy, and it's designed to interfere with the replication of DNA. Yes, they were messing with my genes. This therapy kills the fastest-reproducing cells, including cancer cells.

Gemcitabine conducts guerilla warfare, sneaking into a cell's DNA, leading to cell death. Cisplatin launches a frontal assault, flattening DNA completely, making cell replication impossible. A mighty team! Unfortunately there can be collateral damage. The Gem-Cis combo can affect other cells as well, and I learnt more about those unfortunate conditions soon enough.

I was sent home with a small collection of drugs and a booklet that was a type of personal journal. It was for tracking

---

* Oh yes, the average human bladder will hold up to a half litre, despite what we are led to believe in the opening scene of Austin Powers, International Man of Mystery. The bladder of an African Elephant by contrast can hold up to 18 litres. They whizz up to 50 litres per day.

appointments and medications* and noting any interesting symptoms. I continued with Aprepitant for two days, Ondansetron for three, to control any nausea. I also consumed a steroid called dexamethasone for three days after treatment. Dexamethasone boosts the little Gem-Cis assassins on their deadly mission. I was told that the anti-nausea drugs, while vital for my comfort, were likely to cause constipation. So I went home and took lots of senna.

---

10 July, 2019

During our visit to Camber Sands the previous weekend we stopped in the historic town of Rye, and nipped into a shop called The Tiny Book Store. It was indeed tiny, not much larger than a modern water closet, and in it I found a very tiny book. It was a 150 year old pocket edition 'Of the Imitation of Christ' by Thomas à Kempis with a disintegrating leather cover.

For £5 I now own 328 pages of pure genius right out of the fifteenth century. You may not be familiar with Kempis, but you know his sayings: 'For man proposes, but God disposes'; 'And when he is out of sight, quickly also he is out of mind'; 'Remember that lost time does not return.'

As it turned out, Kempis was a perfect companion for the journey I was about to take. I wasn't walking this road

* I spent quite some time researching these medications while writing this book (I didn't bother during treatment for reasons mentioned previously). I have to hand it to all the little internet algorithms. They really have my number. I'm now getting adverts offering to tell me more about 'Five Herbs For Weak Urine Flow!' and 'Walk With Confidence: Avoid Leaking!' There are also the inevitable 'One Weird Trick' ads. Who knew there was medical click-bait? I suppose it's marginally better than getting adverts for Erectile Dysfunction pills. Or adult diapers. Just sayin'.

alone; the doubt was gone (thanks to Chambers), but I was still wrestling with the fear that if chemotherapy didn't work, my insides might be seriously modified by the surgeon's blade. I found absolutely no peace with this. Kempis had an answer, and I hated it.

'Greater grace shall be added to thee the moment thou hast resigned thyself, and hast not resumed thy claim.' Well ain't that a kick in the head. I read it again, translating it into modern English. 'You will be at peace when you surrender, and stop making unreasonable demands.'

Kempis also asked a tough question: 'Lord, how often shall I resign myself, and wherein shall I forsake myself?' And then he gave me a tougher answer: 'Always and at every hour; as well in small things as in great. The sooner thou doest this, the better it will be with thee; and the more fully and sincerely thou doest it, so much more shall thou please Me, and so much the greater shall be thy gain.' I didn't need to modernise that one to know what it meant.

Most hateful of all was his warning about starting with good intentions about accepting the re-plumbing of my insides, but then putting conditions on it. Even worse, Kempis said, would be giving in to the temptation of trying to do things my own way, or by my own strength. These lead only to my abject failure, or as he put it, 'no progress in the ways of virtue'. Ugh.

I believed Father Kempis. He spoke the truth. But this truth really sucked, and it cut me like the surgeon's knife would. I *couldn't* take his advice. I *wouldn't* take his advice, I *did* have conditions. I could not be cut open. I would not. I wasn't ready to consider anything else, no matter what Kempis said.

God was still sending me a message, and I still refused to listen.

---

12 July, 2019

The prediction about constipation was accurate. Despite regular doses of senna, my intestinal tract was like the worst Los Angeles freeway on a Friday afternoon. We were goin' nowhere fast. We had eight lanes of nothing. It was as though my anus had been surgically removed.

To my limited delight, the other end of my alimentary canal was very happy. I had no nausea, and the dexamethasone steroid stimulated my appetite. But there was much more going in than coming out, and at some point, something would have to give. It was potentially very ugly.

In addition to thinking that I must somehow lay an egg, I was poked at continually by God about the idea of surrender. Yesterday I'd listened to a talk about how Christians need to keep the unity of the Spirit. The speaker taught from Ephesians 4:13, that we should grow toward 'the full and complete standard of Christ.'* I didn't think I was measuring up to much, especially after the confrontation from Father Kempis.

Ephesians 4 was still on my mind when I awoke this morning, so I poured my coffee and studied through it for a while. Afterwards, I opened Oswald Chambers to read my daily devotional from him. The entry for July 12 was based on the book of Ephesians, chapter four, verse thirteen. Another stunning non-coincidence. When God is working hard to make me see something and have me know that He is involved, He gets obvious. Really obvious. Like, two-by-four between the eyes obvious.

---

* A little more Theology 101 if you need it. In last week's episode, Jesus rose from the dead and, after 40 days, ascended to heaven telling his disciples to go hang out in Jerusalem. They did, and when the Holy Spirit showed up they had a big party, evangelising thousands and causing all sorts of ruckus. That third person of the Trinity, the one most people know the least about, is the one Christians carry inside them after they're born again. Holy Spirit, the Spirit of Christ, is that little voice inside that helps me grow to be more like Jesus. Except for those times when I bolt and run the other way.

Chambers hit me with this: 'To fulfil God's perfect design for me requires my total surrender – complete abandonment of myself to Him. Whenever I only want things for myself, the relationship is distorted.' Those words rang in my head: *Total Surrender!* If I prayed only for the future I find *acceptable* (radiotherapy), I risk missing something greater He may have in mind for me because of surgery.

Great, thanks a lot, I moaned. Then I was reminded of Nick Vijicic, born with no fully formed limbs. Nick Vijicic is a head on a torso. He's a powerful speaker with a powerful message. He has a mighty faith, and lives with a tremendous amount of joy. His life of *total surrender* is proof that God supplies sufficient grace for whatever we face. Should I expect any less?

---

13 July, 2019

Total surrender may work, but my bowels still didn't, until today. You may want to skip this entry, where constipation came to an end. It wasn't relief, per se. It wasn't like a sunrise on a warm spring day with a gentle breeze and lots of birdsong backed by Beethoven's Pastoral Symphony. No, it was a transition into long months of 'bowel management,' new territory for Captain Regular.

I awoke with an urgency *('Hooray! At last!')*. This was short-lived and resulted in an occasion of brief spasmodic disappointment before receding into a pile of non-defecatory despair. These incidents punctuated the first nine hours of the day, coming with increasing frequency – like birth contractions. Finally, about 3:00 p.m. I sat down and in the space of 20 minutes very painfully passed what I could only imagine was a hiking boot.

The anti-nausea pills were to blame, they said. They function by moving food more quickly out of the stomach and into the intestines, giving the stomach less to think about. The food is less digested when it arrives in the bowel, which then tends to clog.

I didn't begin taking senna soon enough in the chemo cycle. Lesson learnt. Happily, continuous senna use kept me from locking up entirely. Unhappily, it was often touch and go (no pun intended), even with increased fibre consumption. I apologise that I can't promise this will be the last time defecation drops in (no pun intended) as a topic.

---

16 July, 2019

Cycle One, Day Eight.

This was a shorter day than Day One. I didn't even have to pack a lunch. Last week I over-packed. A large lunch, my laptop, a bible and notebooks, a prayer shawl that was knitted for me, a collection of the New York Times Sunday crossword puzzles thoughtfully sent by my sister Linda. Again today, the pills. Again, the shot of saline, to be followed by the Gemcitabine chaser. Lurch and I made our usual trips together.

It was a warm sunny day, and as I stared out across south London, I pondered how I got here. Not here, as in London here. I wrote about that elsewhere. But here, as in cancer treatment here. Ah yes, 'Why me?' again reared its ugly head as a powerless reaction to what Kempis and Chambers had thrown in my face last week. And to that cosmic howling 'why' there's no 'because'. There's no answer. It's a mystery.

I fell into a doze and then REM sleep, and had a vivid dream. I was on Facebook, writing out a post telling everyone of my total deliverance from cancer, and about the amazing level of health to which I've been restored. When I awoke, Lurch and I toddled off to the loo. Each time we did this I was curious to see what would come out. This had been a constant ritual since that watershed day in April. I'm long used to seeing little red things, clots that break off the still-healing surgical site within my bladder. And I've seen nothing for some days. This time, something brown came out and adhered to the bowl, and I peered closely at it. It was a scab. My surgical wound had finally scabbed over. I was healing.

---

17 July, 2019

Melanie had been in the habit in recent days of waking up consistently between 5:13 and 5:15. That was odd so she asked the Lord about it, and He flooded her with Scripture. Each one was about God's light, or about divine healing.

Matthew 5:13-15 is the famous passage about Christians being salt and light – a light to a dark world. Even in my current situation, I'm to share the Gospel.

Mark 5:13-15 is about the healing of the Gadarene demoniac.

Luke 5:13-15 tells the story of Jesus cleansing (healing) a leper.

John 5:13-15 concludes the story of Jesus' healing at the pool of Bethesda. He comes upon the man later in the temple and says, 'See, you have become whole. Sin no more lest something worse happens to you.'

Paul writes in Ephesians 5:13-15 about us as children of light, saying 'all things are exposed when they are revealed by the light.' I am admonished here to walk carefully, not as a fool, but as a wise man.

Then, dramatically, comes James in his epistle, chapter five, verses 13-15:

'Is anyone among you suffering? Let him pray. Is anyone merry? Let him sing psalms. Is anyone sick among you? Let him call for the elders of the church, and let them pray over him, anointing him with oil in the name of the Lord. And the prayer of faith will save the sick, and the Lord will raise him up. And if he has committed any sins, he will be forgiven.'

I had to take these all as messages designed to strengthen my faith.

Let's close with 1 John 5:13-15. He puts a cap on it all with the ultimate reassurance: 'I have written these things to you who believe in the name of the Son of God, that you may know that you have eternal life, and that you may continue to believe in the name of the Son of God. This is the confidence that we have in Him, that if we ask anything according to His will, He hears us. So if we know that He hears whatever we ask, we know that we have whatever we asked of Him.'

OK God, I'm asking. I'm asking. Please tell me that I'm asking for the right things.

---

18 July, 2019

I asked, He answered. Melanie and I had long been scheduled to attend a three-day conference in Bradford called the European Leaders Alliance (ELA). As graduates of BSSM, we rated a discount ticket. For this, we were given the privilege of ministering in the conference Encounter Room, where people would come for prayer and worship.

I received notice from Guy's that my second round of chemotherapy would *not* begin on Tuesday, 30 July, as originally scheduled. This would have come on the middle day of this conference. Instead, it will be delayed a week to the following Monday, 5 August. We were free to travel.

I asked, He answered.

---

24 July, 2019

Holy Communion had been on my mind these past weeks. When I was growing up in church, I had the idea that communion was just a ritual thing, a religious thing. It wasn't until many decades later that I began to see the richness and the depth of celebrating Jesus' death on the cross. I began to understand it as a celebration of the blood covenant between the Father and the Son.

Isaiah said it best, prophesying that Christ would be wounded for our transgressions and bruised for our iniquities so that 'by his stripes we are healed.'* My healing – spiritual, emotional, mental and physical – exists only as a result of His death and resurrection.

At the communion table, I'm to remember this. Jesus paid for my healing with His death. It's my right to claim what He offers as a free gift. As author George Calleja put it, 'Jesus is there...in the Eucharist, waiting for them to come to Him and ask for His healing...to ask Him 'Heal my wounds.' †

---

* See Isaiah 53:4-5 and 1 Peter 2:24

† Heal My Wounds, George Calleja, (2017)

When I approach the communion table I have nothing. When I leave, I have everything.

---

28 July, 2019

On the smooth ride to Bradford for the ELA conference, I revelled in the pastoral scenes flashing by the train window. It's nice to be out of the city. I enjoyed the years I spent raising sheep, and the thousands upon thousands of them happily cropping grass as they fly past lift my spirit. I want to be like them. Carefree, with an ignorance that surely gives them bliss. Ignorant of the things that trouble me. Blissful from accepting the Biblical promise that, despite my fears, God will make everything that happens during this season work for my good.

Bradford was home for many years to the famed healing evangelist Smith Wigglesworth, and I pondered his legacy as we hurtled northward at 80 miles per hour. Wigglesworth didn't begin full-time ministry until his late 40s. His schooling had been so poor he learnt to read in adulthood by studying the Bible. It's said that's the only book he ever read, or allowed into his house.

It certainly shaped his attitude: 'I'm not moved by what I see or hear,' he famously said, 'I am moved by what I believe!' As the train pulled into Bradford station and I jerked our cases off the rack, I thought 'That's easy for you to say, Brother Wigglesworth.' My faith, while growing, was not *that* strong. Not just yet.

Freshly in town, it was time to fill the larder at our AirBnb. We dove out of a pouring northern rain into Tesco Express. We moved through the aisles behind the squish, squish, squish of a limping young man named Ben. He was soaked to the skin, and his rucksack was the same. Afterwards, the three of us stood under a bus shelter together, waiting for the storm to let up. Ben had been thrown out of work, which had thrown him out on the street.

The squishing of his feet came from trainers with holes in the sides. His feet hurt, and he limped because he was in tremendous pain. We helped him a bit financially and prayed for his feet, for provision, and for a job. As we made our way to the apartment, I told the Lord if I saw him again when the shops were open, I'd buy him a pair of shoes.

That night I had a powerful dream. Endless waves of healing power washed over me, like it was a direct visitation from the Lord, or from a healing angel. I awoke to find that in my sleep, I had laid hands on my abdomen, right over my bladder.

---

30 July, 2019

It's good to see friends in unexpected places, and finding Steve Brown at ELA was a treat. Steve and I had served together on a Healing and Pastoral Care team at BSSM. As soon as I shared my medical news he introduced his friend Irene Grainger, who had recovered from cancer, miraculously she would say. Cancer UK statistics would give Irene a much smaller chance of recovery than mine. Irene told me she had an encounter during radiotherapy where she sensed heavenly hands laid on her for healing, much like in my dream the night before. She also had an angelic encounter.

There's incredible power in these testimonies, and many Christians believe they can be prophetic as well. If nothing else they provide massive encouragement! Revelation says 'Worship only God! For the essence of prophecy is to give a clear witness for Jesus.'* So, when I hear a testimony of someone healed of cancer, or who had a miraculous experience during treatment, it reminds me that if God did it once, He can do it again.

God also puts people together who can benefit from each other's testimony. I'd last seen Steve on another continent 15 months before and had no idea he'd be at ELA. Yet, it 'just so happened' that he was not only there, but was friends with Irene, who was also present, and who had a personal victory that fit what I was praying for. The odds are very long against these being random events, but if you want to call them coincidence, I won't stop you. Just keep reading. Perhaps by the end of the book you'll choose another term for them.

I received another vision, this time during worship at ELA. I was walking across a balance beam, something I doubt I could do in real life – the ball of my foot is wider than the beam itself! Nevertheless, there I was, and when I reached the middle, I stopped. I leant over as far as I wished in any direction, but didn't fall off. My feet remained firmly connected to the bar as I swayed back and forth. A short poem leapt into my mind.

My heart is a trumpet,
Listen to it sing.
My heart is a torch,
Watch it burn.
'I gave you feet for a reason,
Now, use them to follow Me.'

---

* Revelation 19:10b (NLT), which also suggests that the essence of prophecy 'is the message confirmed by Jesus.' The Bible says prophecies must be tested (see 1 Thessalonians 5:20-21, which says 'Do not despise prophecies but test everything; hold fast what is good.' See also 2 Peter 3:16, 1 Cor 14:29, 32) It's also mandatory that as someone willing to receive the prophetic that I live in a prophetic culture and submit myself to solid spiritual authority that does the same. (Acts 20:29-30). Many of the prophetic words I've received have been confirmed or fit into a pattern subsequently proven through the events of my life. I wait expectantly on the remainder.

We asked the Faithful Pray-ers for something different this week: For me: wisdom to know what I need and the courage to ask for it. For Melanie: discernment, to take every negative thought captive, and to renounce fear. Not every battle is waged on a physical front. Some are strictly spiritual.

---

31 July, 2019

It was our last full day at ELA, and the weather had improved. It was cool for late July, but the sky was clearing, and it promised to be fair by afternoon. As we walked the mile through Bradford to the church we saw Ben – now in high spirits. The morning after we met him at Tesco, someone had come by and bought him a new pair of shoes.

Each day of the conference saw larger numbers of people coming to the Encounter Room. Many of them asked for healing prayer, and we saw God deliver cessation of pain from knees, shoulders and other joints, and even an end to one man's hearing loss. As we neared the end of the afternoon session, one of the men I'd been ministering with, Mark Zechin, handed me a folded piece of paper. It had a drawing of a warrior pulling back an arrow in a large bow. The text below it read, 'There is a very specific target to the core of what you are dealing with – the Lord is directly pointing His angels to fire directly and purposefully to this very specific target – the centre of the issue!'

Mark had no knowledge that I was undergoing chemotherapy and praying for radiotherapy as follow-up. The doubt I'd been carrying about that began to fade. I immediately saw this as a message about radiotherapy, which of course is a *targeted* therapy.

The journey from doubt to faith always takes me from wishing to knowing. Doubt has me ask, 'Wouldn't it be great if healing happened?' Faith has me say, 'Isn't it great that God's word about healing is true?'

When I stepped into the prophetic life, two things happened. The theoretical *knowing* of God's truth became much more clear, while the practical discerning of that truth was often hazy. In the prophetic life, faith must lead, not follow. Also, the markers have to be clear before I can take action. There can be a lot of waiting involved.

The Bible records that God often instructs people to wait for Him. It's not that He's late for dinner, or wants to make an entrance, rather He shows up in His own time, so we'll realise that what we desire truly comes from Him. His patience is greater than mine, and when I jump the gun, when I get ahead of Him as it were, He may not show up at all. And so I get to start again, and wait. When I wait long enough, He does show up, and it's always just in the nick of time, His time.

---

2 August, 2019

Melanie and I are back at Guy's Hospital again today, this time headed to the Urology Centre. It's at the end of a long and spacious corridor lined with posters encouraging those of us being treated for cancer to, in their secular way, 'Fear Not!' The very last of them, next to the Urology Centre entry, had a picture of my prophetic archer on it.

His name is Tony. His nocked arrow points at me. His determined gaze stands behind the powerful fist gripping the bow. His tattooed fingers spell L I F E. The slogan above reads, 'Together, we can target cancer.' As in *a very specific target, the centre of the issue*. I'm stunned, but not surprised, at the ways in which God continues to speak.

Before checking in at the Urology Centre, we stopped and I dug around in my backpack. I just happened to have my notebook in there, which contained the prophetic picture Mark had given me two days before. I held it up next to Tony and we snapped a picture.

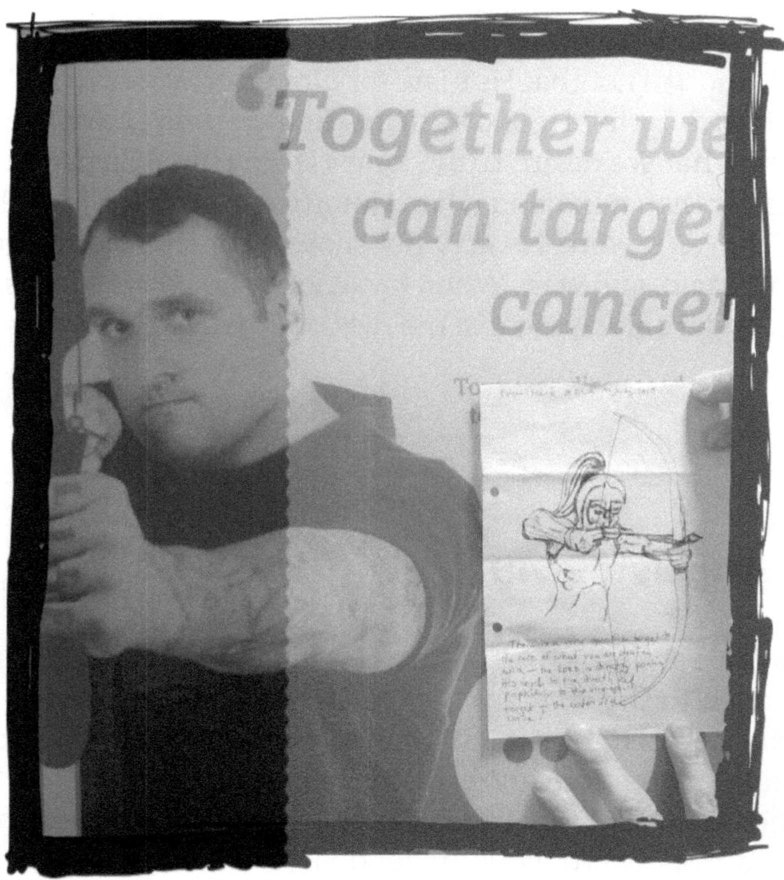

There was also good news from the MRI review with Dr. Brio. The scans taken before chemotherapy began showed no cancer outside the bladder. It was a T-2 tumour. High fives all around. Things were headed in the right direction! Radiotherapy was still on the table, IF the chemotherapy adequately shrank the tumour. I'd have another round of scans, after my second course of chemo was complete. The decision about radiotherapy would come after that.

My faith grew but I continued to struggle with the idea of surgery (as though it were truly my decision). I leant on the short version of Reinhold Niebuhr's *Serenity Prayer*, which I learnt back when I was attending AA meetings.

'God, grant me the serenity to accept the things I cannot change, the courage to change the things I can, and the wisdom to know the difference.' That prayer was written backward. I always needed wisdom first. If I didn't have wisdom, how could I discern between what I must change and what to leave alone? The courage to act and the peace to accept can only follow the wisdom to know.

I remembered one of the most definitive Bible verses about wisdom. 'Pride leads to disgrace but with humility comes wisdom.' * Ouch. I wasn't making the wrong request, but making it out of order. If I wanted wisdom, I needed to humble myself, because if I didn't, I knew God would. He had done it before, and it had not been pleasant. I had to make my peace, not with Him, but with my fear.

Our meeting with Dr. Brio was a check-in more than a check-up. We reviewed statistics about radiotherapy and cancer recurrence rates. These are complicated and based on many factors including age, stage of cancer and type of treatment. Actuarial experts believe my odds of living ten more years if I have radiotherapy are slightly better than 50-50. However, the doctor told me, 5% of male patients still need surgery. 40% suffer loss of potency.

I interrupted him. 'Wait a minute,' I said. 'Let's look at this a different way. How about we say 95% *don't* require surgery and 60% retain full sexual function?' Blink, blink. Brio barely missed a beat. 'That's a great outlook!' His grin widened. 'Look on the bright side!'

To his credit, from then on, he always announced any statistic in a positive manner. I like him more for this. After all, death and life are in the power of the tongue.

---

* Proverbs 11:2 (NLT)

4 August, 2019

After the full 21-day chemotherapy cycle, I took stock. I'd had no nausea or sickness, only a slight dizziness if I moved my head too quickly in one direction. My bowels were mostly under control and I was not fatigued. My appetite was robust and I got outside to walk regularly. I could run for a bus. I was in no pain. It's full summer and the weather was glorious. I was receiving free state-of-the-art health care. I'm an old hand at this! Life was good. But that was going to change soon.

---

5 August, 2019

It was yet another sunny day, which I enjoyed through the full-sized windows of Chemotherapy Suite B at Guy's Cancer-Free Centre. I was back in the chair for another long day with Lurch. Round Two, Day One. This was routine already: the same front-loading of my bladder; the taking of my vitals, my personal details recited again and again to ensure they match my wrist band and the records. The lunch bag, the Bible and notebook, the crosswords.

Melanie had a picture during prayer the previous day of my medication drip being the Liquid Life of Jesus pouring into me. I leant back in the chair and closed my eyes. I focused on that image, the idea of life replacing death. I became lost in the 'tik, tik, tik' of Lurch's pump. 'Drip, drip, drip,' it said. Then, dramatically I heard this chorus: 'Life, life, life.'

In my mind's eye I saw liquid life drip-dropping into my vein, each drop diffusing out into individual molecules. I saw them swimming and spinning through the bloodstream on the way to their cellular destinations. I was a sponge absorbing this treatment, becoming super-saturated to overflowing.

The good flowed in, the bad flowed out. Life came to replace death. I floated in the transition from bad necrosis to good necrosis. I dozed in the afternoon sunshine, wrapped in a prayer shawl knitted by my step-mother Ruth's group. It had arrived in time for Round One of Chemotherapy back in July. The card that came with it read:

'This shawl was knit *in prayer* especially for you and has been blessed by people at St. Paul's. It is saturated with love and blessings. Whenever you wrap in it, pull it onto your lap or see it lying around, may it remind you of God's infinite care and keeping.' I fell further into sleep. 'Tik, tik, tik. Drip, drip, drip. Life, life, life.' But the dozing didn't last long. Soon, much too soon, it was time to take Lurch for another stroll.

---

12 August, 2019

Round Two, Day Eight, a short day. Each time that I had chemotherapy I was held up until the nurses checked my blood work. Giving blood has become a routine like everything else. But, as the weeks marched by, I became less of a phlebotomist's dream, and more of a voodoo doll. The sharp scratches are becoming sharper.

It was almost as though my veins were melting into my arms. They no longer pulsed with vigour and life; they were flat and sallow, more difficult to locate. After a blood draw or hours with a cannula, my arms would bruise, as though they'd been punched repeatedly by a cantankerous garden gnome.

The Gem-Cis drug combo attacked more than just my tumour. It was *not* a targeted therapy. All my fast-growing membranes suffered. These included all the epithelial cells, like the ones that line the alimentary canal (from the mouth all the way through the gut) and the blood vessels, among many others. That's why it took increasing levels of skill to find a vein and keep it from collapsing while blood was drawn. It also explained why my constipation (which I finally got under control) now threatened to turn to diarrhoea. All my linings were stressed out.

Too much of the time I still wrestled with the horrifying idea of surgery to preserve my life. I was convinced it threatened one of my favourite things: my love of being outdoors. I'm happiest in the natural world, hiking, camping, backpacking, even just standing in the rain (a frequent option here in London). No matter that the experts say I can live a completely normal and active life with a bag strapped to my waist, I'm somehow not sure I believe them. Perhaps I just didn't want to.

Remember the company with 11 types of catheter bags? There are even more options for bladder-less types who are constantly on-the-go (no pun intended). These have compelling names like 'Urine Drain Bag' and 'Deluxe Urinary Drain Bag' and even 'Bedside Drainage Bag With SplashGuard (Complete With Sampling Port and Universal Hangar).' This is proof positive that good marketing jobs exist in every field.

My body already has enough stomata,* I thought. Do I really want an artificial one added to the mix? My -ectomy resulting in an -ostomy, as it were. No really, doctor, I incysto-, please don't.†

* A stoma (plural stomata) is any opening of the body, such as your mouth, nose or water works.

† 10 points for Gryffindor if you got the joke. If not, go here: https://en.wikipedia.org/wiki/List_of surgical_procedures (accessed 1 April, 2020)

Then I did what I should have done at the beginning. I looked for stories of people who had experience with this type of surgery. Thanks to MacMillan Cancer Support there are shedloads.* Every patient is unique, of course, and I sorted through many threads to find people with positive attitudes. They were out there. Thriving was possible.

13 August, 2019

It's a pleasantly warm and sunny English afternoon with puffy clouds and a light breeze. Melanie and I are out for a walk. She found a spring on the ground.

14 August, 2019

Today provided a rare treat for an American Baseball fan living in Britain. Major League Baseball had made arrangements for a dozen or so of its 'Game of the Week' broadcasts to be streamed live on YouTube. My beloved Minnesota Twins were playing an afternoon game, which meant a reasonable early evening hour in London. Melanie fired it up on the telly and it came on at the beginning of an interview with Twins pitcher Devin Smeltzer.

* https://www.macmillan.org.uk/

The first question for Smeltzer was about being healed from cancer. Make that bladder cancer. He was diagnosed age nine with a rare cancer called pelvic rhabdomyosarcoma, centred in his bladder. Good news! His treatment was successful, and he's been completely healthy since then. Once again, I'm stunned.

What are the odds my team is in the game of the week? Pretty good, with 30 teams and a dozen match-ups. What are the odds I'd hear about the game being on YouTube? Not bad, considering I'm a rabid Twins fan. What are the odds its a day game, meaning I can easily watch it? 62 out of 162 is just over 1-in-3. Almost betting odds.

What are the odds they are interviewing Devin Smeltzer? 1 in 26, about 4%. Maybe smaller, considering he's not even the starting pitcher in this 6-5 loss to the Milwaukee Brewers. What are the odds I tune in at that moment? The odds Smeltzer had cancer? The odds that it was bladder cancer? You go figure. It makes my head hurt, unless I accept that it's not a coincidence. Then, and only then, can I rest easy.

---

19 August, 2019

The delay for Round Two of chemotherapy not only made our trip to Bradford possible, but also a long-planned holiday in Cornwall.* The third week of each chemotherapy cycle (days 15-21) is for rest; there's nothing on the medical schedule. This was yet another answer to prayer. We'd made our Cornwall booking long before treatment began, and left it to God as to whether the trip would happen. We booked in faith, and He answered.

---

* Just like 8 million of the other 9 million people in Greater London.

The long-reserved stone farmhouse annexe near Porkellis* appeared very quaint online, all the south-west coast was supposedly within an hour's drive, and the weather prediction was glorious. Before we left that Monday, it was back to Guy's for the aforementioned CT and MRI scans. These are critical to what happens after chemotherapy. From my medical record:

The key determinants for delivering radical radiotherapy are firstly that there is a good functioning bladder; secondly there are no contraindications to radiotherapy; and thirdly there has been an excellent response to chemotherapy. He fulfils the first 2 criteria, and I have requested a repeat CT and MRI...to assess the response. If there is an excellent response we can then arrange radical chemoradiotherapy when we next meet. (emphasis mine).

It was unpleasant having untold levels of toxins swirling around in my body doing only God knew what. The combination of steroids *(up, up, up!)* and slow poisoning *(down, down, down!)* created a stretched-out sensation. This peaked about day seven, and then slowly receded through day twenty-one. Sometimes it was as though I didn't know my own body any more.

Time was I could predict my capacity for this or that physical activity, and knew instinctively when it was time to stop and rest. That had all been blown away. Now, when I became tired, I was *immediately* tired and came to a forced halt, no matter where I was or what I was doing. When I remembered to focus on God as a comforter, instead of my own discomfort, it was better. Even when when my plate had a crap sandwich on it, I could still be filled with joy. And I always heard from my Faithful Pray-ers, just when I needed to.

Thank you Father that you are giving Alan life through Jesus' death and resurrection. We know you can multiply and increase natural offerings, like loaves and fishes, and we believe you can increase the effectiveness of chemotherapy. So we bless the medicine in Alan's body to increase and multiply in this resting

* I know. It is reminiscent of a sandwich.

period, to supernaturally seek out and destroy all cancer cells in his body. Continue to bestow on Alan a deep and profound faithfulness and obedience. Cast out all the cancer in Alan's body. We pray for this next round of treatment that you would multiply its healing with your glorious, relentless power. In Jesus' mighty name Amen.

I lay in the MRI and the CT scanners that morning staring at nothing. I concentrated on what the Pray-ers said, handled the truth of it, turned it over again and again. I weighed that all against how I felt. The sensations in my body needed to be irrelevant. The health of my heart and soul must count for more.

Father Kempis kept speaking to me as we motored out of London to the south-west. 'Greater grace shall be added to thee the moment thou hast resigned thyself, and hast not resumed thy claim.' As the suburbs gave way to exurbs and we flew back in time past Stonehenge on Salisbury Plain, I left the hospital and treatment behind. Back there somewhere too was expectation.

Hope I had with me. Hope that my body would remain in one piece through this trial. Hope that God would help me figure out what I could change, and what I could not. Also, that He would give me the wisdom to know the difference.

---

20 August, 2019

We drove as far as East Devon that Monday, and spent the night at Weycroft Hall. It's a stunning Grade I building with the oldest portion, the Great Hall, hailing from about 1400 AD. It was well-restored in the 19th century* and now houses Weycroft Ministries, hosted by Vince and Clio Turner. Our friends Tim

* https://britishlistedbuildings.co.uk/101098625-weycroft-hall-axminster# (accessed 1 Apr, 2020)

and Ruth Boxer and their children also live there. We know the Boxers from our year at BSSM, and we spent a happy evening reconnecting, sharing a meal, and swapping news. The Boxers know more than just a little about living by faith. They followed God's call to move halfway across the world for a year with seven children, and no clear financial path.

God took care of their needs from end to end, and it was encouraging to recount those stories, and then pray together. They are a physical reminder that God doesn't disappoint; He always comes through. For a man like me, working daily to keep doubt and uncertainty at arm's length, it was all like honey on bread.

Before we headed out to Porkellis in the morning, I joined the men, including Tim and Vince, for a prayer meeting. At one point, Vince stared at me and declared, 'You are being *irradiated in the Holy Spirit!*' Tim and I glanced at one another, knowingly. Tim knew what was up with me, of course, but Vince had no prior knowledge of my medical status, nor my intense desire to be targeted for radiotherapy and *not* *not* **not** for surgery.

Again, I was stunned. The springs, the interview with the baseball player, the picture of the archer and it's match-up with the 'Target Cancer' poster. And now this. There's no natural explanation for these 'messages'. They had to be the work of the Holy Spirit.

After our midday drive, Melanie and I found that the rented annexe in Cornwall *was* quaint. Everything we wanted *was* within an hour's drive. The weather *was* glorious. We walked and walked, each day's views topping the last. We walked and walked, something like 30 miles in five days. Cornwall was a much-needed calm before returning back into the storm the following week. But when I got home, I was exhausted. The recliner, and Lurch, were waiting. All too soon, the cycle would begin again.

---

27 August, 2019

Before chemotherapy resumed, we were back at the Urology Centre to review the CT and MRI scans from the week before. It was like a horror film with a tumour as protagonist. If my response was 'excellent', do we move on to radiotherapy? And what *is* 'excellent' anyway? In my mind, it meant the tumour was 100% dissolved, dead, outahere. *'Presto! Now you see it, now you don't!'* And if the response isn't 'excellent', does that mean radiotherapy is out of the question?

Before the review, I gave blood again, for the pre-chemotherapy workup. How are the kidneys this week? Am I dehydrated? How does my immune system look? My liver? The multi-page report is littered with abbreviations like ABG, BUN, RBC and WBC.* When my number was called I crammed into another tiny room with a big chair and a phlebotomist. Like all the others, she asked me how I was doing. I told her I'm being treated for cancer, but I'm healed in Jesus' name. I get various responses to this. Today's response was, 'That's nice, Lovely. Sharp scratch!'

After three failed attempts with the butterfly needle, she sheepishly had to ask a nurse to take my blood. My vein kept collapsing on her. I remained stoic through the pain and silently prayed for her, knowing she felt worse about it than I did. It was disconcerting and painful to watch the plastic tubing bend after the needle went in my arm. It's supposed to just slide right

* ABG is Arterial Blood Gases (not Autogenous Bone Graft). BUN is Blood Urea Nitrogen (not the Bundle file extension). RBC is Red Blood Count (not to be confused with the Royal Bank of Canada). Finally, WBC is White Blood Count (although I would prefer Weird But Cool).

in. It was painful because those blood draw needles are big needles – 18 gauge. Also, gouging around in there, inside the vein, is not nearly as satisfying as, say, picking one's nose.

An 18 gauge needle is a big needle.* By comparison, an insulin needle is probably a 26 or smaller. Even the sheep I once raised rated a 22 for their comfort when they needed an injection. Oh well. Bring on the bruise patrol. Melanie and I prayed our way into the doctor's office. God's resurrection power can take away all cancer, we declared. The scans showed that He hadn't. The tumour had shrunk by only a third after two rounds of chemotherapy.

The doctor claimed this is good. 'You certainly don't want it growing – ha ha!' Very funny, Brio. Very funny. He assured us it will shrink further after more chemotherapy of course, at which point we'll make the final decision about radiotherapy – or surgery.

Thank you, Lord, that you can do more than we could ask or imagine. Give us an expectancy that you will do amazing things for us! Show us how to wait patiently, stay alert to your leading and be prepared to act when you call. Lord, your grace is sufficient for us. Jesus, you are our master. Cancer, you must leave Alan's body in Jesus' name!

---

28 August, 2019

One year ago today, I stepped off a Delta 767 at Heathrow International Airport and set foot on British soil for the first time. Instead of commemorating this by zooming off on a wild,

* The larger the gauge number, the smaller the needle. An 18 gauge needle is 1.27 mm. A 6 gauge needle is more than 5 mm in diameter, while a 34 is less than 0.02 mm. A 6 gauge needle could easily be used for knitting.

romantic celebration, I'm huddled with Lurch, wrapped in my prayer shawl, in the Chemotherapy Village at Guy's Cancer-Free Centre. It takes a Village to toxify a patient. Today is Day One of Round Three.

My side-effects have remained minimal (by comparison to everyone I spoke with, and by the doctors' reckoning), but I sure didn't feel the way I wanted to feel. There was a more definite pattern to this now, a routine for the two weeks I'm infused. Days one through five the steroids make me fly, I'd sleep little, and my bowels worked well enough. Day six was a crash, and I'd begin developing diarrhoea.

Day seven was the worst. Days eight through fifteen were a milder version of the previous week. The rest of each cycle was about resting and recovering, to prepare for the next round. Each cycle the high had been a little higher and the low a little lower. My mood had begun to slip. I became uncharacteristically* cranky.

This third and final round of chemotherapy was punishing. And yet it wasn't the physical punishment of fatigue or sickness or sepsis or blood clots or even the hair loss that so many of us suffer. It was nothing less than a spiritual beat-down. I finally lost my joy, which I'd kept through even the most physically uncomfortable days, even during the passage of the hiking boot.

I'd not been this separated from God since before I surrendered my life to Him. It wasn't even like He was sitting across the room instead of here next to me. He was gone. Vanished. Off the grid. My prayers bounced right off the wall, only to return and slap me in the face. It was like being in an echo chamber with no sound, the worst type of sensory deprivation.

For a full week I moved about as though half-dead. I was in hell. It was the vast emptiness of spiritual nowhere-ness. I believed I was alone. All the prophetic words, the pictures, the signs, the repeated encouragements through dreams,

* Wow! Either seven syllables or eight, depending on whether you pronounce it like an American or not.

all these meant nothing now. I began asking myself if these things were even real. Had I been making all this up? Storm clouds appeared to be gathering. It was like being lost in the woods, crying out desperately in fear. 'Dad! Mum! Where are you? Help me!'

The wind was roaring through the trees; a storm was brewing and it was getting dark. I was scared, and God's presence was remote. Very remote. Since my side-effects were truly 'minimal' by everyone else's measurements, then this mustn't be physical. It must be spiritual. So I went to war against the devil.

---

3 September, 2019

For a full week, the battle continued, and I appeared to be losing. Spiritual punishment became spiritual torture. Moment-to-moment life became brutal and intense. Nothing I'd learnt about spiritual warfare availed. I was standing against the devil, but God did not seem to have my back. True to what I know, I kept asking. *When all else fails, keep asking!* And so I continued to do this, trying to keep the faith.

I remained in this pool of spiritual darkness as I made my way to the Healing Rooms. I was desperate for prayer. I was like a man who'd been treading water for an untold time, a night and a day perhaps, and needed to be pulled out of the ocean, away from certain death. My spirit was exhausted, yet the prayers I received offered no immediate refreshment. My friends had pulled me into the boat, but I still felt like I was thrashing in the water, drowning.

Heading home, I got off the Underground at Clapham Common, moving on auto-pilot. As I emerged and turned out onto the pavement, I saw the word 'Peckham' on the bus pulling up nearby. *That's my bus!* I said to myself, and began jogging. I made it just before the end of the queue filed in, and copped a seat on the upper deck.

So much for auto-pilot. It didn't take long to realise I was on the wrong bus. Just as my usual bus (37) goes to Peckham, so did this 345, but not through my neighbourhood. So, I decanted myself at Stockwell Station, to ride the tube over to Brixton, where I could again catch the 37. As soon as I got off the train and started up the escalator at Brixton Station, I smelled incense, sweet and cloying. As I trudged wearily up the steps to exit, the smell was almost overpowering, and I began to swoon. A street vendor had set up shop right in front of the station, and the air sucked into the underground filled its corridors and chambers with his aromatic advertisement.

Brixton Station's frontage is a hotbed for salesman, vendors, hustlers, dealers, hucksters, beggars, people collecting for charity, people preaching hellfire and damnation. In other words, it was just another afternoon on Brixton Road, and yet I sensed a spiritual darkness over the place. One of the side-effects of chemotherapy *not* mentioned by NHS is an increased sensitivity to spiritual atmospheres. As I physically crumpled within myself week on week, my spirit expanded. Just as a blindfold would make my hearing more acute, the loss of physical stamina improved my spiritual awareness. I can't explain it, only report it.

As I passed the table with burning incense the darkness lifted and I saw a vision in white. She was a compact African woman my own age, in a white robe and a multi-coloured turban. She was beaming, and glowing from inside. She was handing out Christian tracts, and I stopped and took one. I began to encourage her and then shouted, 'You will bring many people into God's kingdom!' Immediately the darkness over me began to lift.

It was as though I had missed the 37 so as to be given this encounter. I wouldn't have passed that way otherwise. It was the first answer to a week of desperate searching and pleading. The second came into my hand from my rucksack when I got back on the 37 in Brixton.

My friend Geoff Rowland had given me a short paper about The Dark Night of the Soul. This is a phenomenon written about by 16th century Spanish mystic St. John of the Cross. Geoff suggested a book on the topic. I bought it and in the coming days, came to understand what I'd been experiencing.

I also remembered Kempis again: 'Greater grace shall be added to thee the moment thou hast resigned thyself, and hast not resumed thy claim.' Maybe the reason I'd been in hell, experiencing no grace, was that I still fiercely gripped my 'claim' about radiotherapy. Perhaps it was time to let go. As I stepped down from the 37 near my home, Christ's words from the book of John rang in my head: 'Rise, take up your bed and walk.'* By the next morning both my spirit and my body began a turnaround.

---

4 September, 2019

Round Three, Day Eight. Things had changed. Melanie was now back at work, teaching, and her absence was almost painful. It also didn't help that I was rewriting a memoir about sexual abuse and spiritual darkness. The book was a demanding presence, often getting in my face and staying

* John 5:8 describes the healing at the pool of Bethesda. 'Jesus said to him, "Rise, take up your bed and walk." Immediately the man was healed, took up his bed, and walked.'

there. I couldn't handle it, and moved at warp speed into season six of Star Trek: Deep Space Nine.

Why did Chief O'Brien have so many crazy things happen to him? O'Brien gets sent off on secret spy missions, is miniaturised, is kidnapped. He watched his own clone buy the farm. O'Brien was once possessed by an alien. In my own darkness, I empathised with him. There were times in that receding dark season when I thought I was the one possessed by an alien. I was in an alien environment at Guy's Cancer-Free Centre, surrounded by aliens in various shades of alien blue.

They're conducting weird alien medical experiments on those of us unfortunate enough to be held captive and strapped into these deceptively comfortable alien easy chairs. This dark fantasy scraped through my mind again as Lurch continued his 'Tik, tik, tik.' I saw the 'Drip, drip, drip', but was not yet fully back to declaring 'Life, life, life.'

And then, out of nowhere, a real live human being – a *free* human being – one not possessed by an alien, walked into the room. It was one of the chaplains, Reverend Joshua Adewumi. As I watched him, time slowed down. He visited one patient, and then the next. Slowly, deliberately. Some engaged in conversation, and he took the time they needed, sitting at their feet on a low stool. Others were uninterested, but he took time for them anyway.

He exuded care. Finally, it was my turn. The small wheeled stool came to rest by my feet right after Lurch and I returned from our most recent trip to the watering hole. I timed this so as to spend as much time with Reverend Joshua as he would allow. I needed his pastoral balm spread on my wounded heart. We spoke. He asked after my condition, my spirit, how my wife was doing. He prayed for me. I prayed for him. We talked about Kempis' greater grace, and about the power of acceptance. We talked of surrender. I poured my heart out. I needed to confess my fear.

He reminded me that Christ engaged in complete trust when he died at Calvary, and said I should do the same. *Trust the Father*. That was Christ's gig on the cross. Look where it got Him! Reverend Joshua reminded me before he left that God's love is unconditional, and my trust in Him must be unconditional too. Just like Kempis did. Later in the day, when all was done, I said goodbye to Lurch for the last time, went home and prayed, and tried to surrender.

<u>Prayer Quiver</u>

Prayers are the arrows of the warrior,
Not aimed at the enemy's heart,
But shot into the air.

Under attack from my enemy,
I fire arrows into God's throne room,
The messages tied around the shafts.

They fall at His feet,
He picks them up and reads them,
He adds them to His collection.

Just as He saves our tears,
He saves our prayers,
They last for all time.

'Stand against the enemy', He says,
'But don't be mute like small-g gods.
Stand and pray in My image.'

Fire round after round,
As many as it takes because,
He will never let your quiver go empty.

---

6 September, 2019

This was another D-Day: Decision Day. Chemotherapy was done. What would come next? Melanie took time off work for today's meeting. Dr. Brio ran through the scan information again. 30% shrinkage after two rounds of chemotherapy was encouraging, but not overly promising. I wasn't ready to decide what came next. We entered the consultation room bearing the weight of all the medical advice, but also were buoyed up by what we believed God had been saying. The springs. The prophetic picture of the archer. The word about being *irradiated in the Holy Spirit.*

We believed the truth of God's word was more powerful than doctor's information, and we continued to have faith for divine healing. We'd seen it in others, but also recognised that temporal medicine may be our path. My Healing Room mentors are fond of reminding us that medicine is good. 'There's no second-class healing,' they say. I wanted to surrender to the possibility of surgery, but it was hard. I was still afraid.

(Insert big indecisive Christian gulp here)

Whatever was to come, we knew the Lord would give us sufficient grace for anything we might encounter. We'd seen that before also. It had to be enough consolation for now. 'We've seen some shrinkage of the tumour,' the doctor said, 'but not as much as we'd like to see. Often, the response to chemotherapy is more dramatic.'

'So, 30% reduction after two rounds of chemo – how much after this last one, do you think?' I asked.

'It's hard to say. Routinely we scan after two because we want to make a decision about the next treatment option as soon as possible after round three. We don't want to wait another two weeks for scans and then a review. We want to crack right on with it. These tumours can be persistent, and we know from years of clinical data that surgical removal of the bladder is the surest option to stop any spread of cancer beyond the initial site.'

'What do *you* recommend?' I asked, aware he wouldn't bite, that it was up to us. Instead, he said, 'I know you want to avoid the surgical option, but it is, percentage-wise, your best bet.' We needed to decide today. Melanie and I looked at one another.

'I understand you'll want to talk this over. We're in clinic for a while yet. How about you take some time – half an hour? I'll see you straight away when you're ready.'

We left the consultation room and headed outside because the weather was good. As we slipped past Tony, still drawing his bow to 'target cancer,' I again noticed the tattoos across his knuckles: L I F E. That's what I wanted to hold onto. Life. But what would it cost?

We wandered down and out of Guy's, past London Bridge Station and through Hays Galleria, once a warehouse and wharf, now a glass-topped shopping arena. We very quickly found ourselves standing on the bank of the Thames. The river's historic name, Tamesas, is believed to have meant 'darkness'. Its water slipped past us and around the HMS Belfast, moored permanently nearby. The water wasn't dark today, not like the cloud enveloping my heart.

The early afternoon sun was sharp against the water as it beamed down upstream of us to the west. I was afraid to look into it, into what might be coming. It was too painful to take in. I could only look downstream, down to where things were flowing beyond my grasp. Melanie and I had a short conversation, prayed, and made our decision. But mostly, I just watched the water until it was time to turn back.

Once more in the consultation room, I said, 'We want to move to radiotherapy.' Melanie was sitting close now, holding my hand. I was outwardly calm, if still inwardly unsettled. The doctor pushed his chair back and scratched his head.

'There is one other thing we can try,' he said, much to our surprise. 'You know the standard of care here: two rounds of chemo, scans and then a quick decision?' We nodded.

He continued breezily. 'There is one treatment facility here in the UK that gives *three* rounds of chemo before the scans, and then a fourth round.' Melanie and I squeezed our hands together, but didn't beak his gaze. Not yet.

'You've tolerated the chemotherapy so well, what if you have a fourth round of chemo and *then* we scan you again?'

Now Melanie and I looked at one another, smiling, nodding. What was this? An exception to every rule we had heard about! Not just two-rounds-and-scan before the third. Not just three-rounds-and-scan before the fourth. But four-rounds-and-scan before decision time. We quickly agreed to this plan. I would unexpectedly be reunited with Lurch Monday week.

As we turned into the corridor once again, I winked at Tony, still bending his bow, and issued a silent prayer of thanks.

---

13 September, 2019

My dream life had been vivid and crazy. I had a hole in my hand. I saw all the way into my body, which was filled with light, and so I gazed upon my tumour. I saw my capillaries. In my imagination I ordered more of them to be built, to reverse the bad necrosis. More capillaries would feed the tumour more blood, and more chemotherapy.

I heard Psalm 51: 'Create in me a clean heart, O God, and renew a right spirit within me. Restore me to the joy of Your salvation, and uphold me with Your willing spirit.'* And then

---

* Psalm 51:10, 12

I woke up. Right after breakfast, those same verses turned up in the book I was reading. Later, I was prompted to listen to a particular teaching on healing I'd forgotten I had. The speaker built the message around those same verses from Psalm 51, and my watchword verses from Isaiah 35:

'3 Strengthen the weak hands, and support the feeble knees. 4 Say to those who are of a fearful heart, "Be strong, fear not. Your God will come with vengeance, even God with a recompense; He will come and save you."'

I got the message. A clean heart (from humbling myself in repentance) is what sets me right. Then I'm returned to the joy of salvation. And *then* God comes and saves me. It was a process, and I was, at long last, ready to begin.

---

16 September, 2019

Round Four, Day One. Guy's chaplaincy will bring the Eucharist into a ward at a patient's request. As I continued recovering from my Dark Night, and realised I'd be back in chemotherapy, I knew I needed it. I grew up in a church that was more about following rules than having a personal relationship with Jesus. I shed it like skin as I moved into young adulthood. But in my 50s I was born again, with what's called a 'charismatic' faith – one that not only worships the Father and follows Jesus, but also seeks a personal relationship with the Holy Ghost.

As someone who is open to signs and prophecies, who prays and sings in tongues, I want to hear from God. I tend to worship with wild abandon. It's hard to keep me in my seat during church. I laugh, cry and sing. I find joy in God's word. I have true love in the company of believers. This is all vastly different from the ritualised church of my youth. Sit still. Be quiet. Sing in unison. Stand when everyone stands. Kneel when everyone kneels. Don't question anything. Conformity to the religion is good. Anything that bucks tradition is bad (they wouldn't have said *demonic* or *heretical*, but rather *shameful*).

Moving from the U.S. to Great Britain at age 62 and attending an Anglican church was a bit of a shock. There are *charismata*, but also plenty of tradition. It was surprisingly comforting and familiar. It was as though God had returned as a gift something I had wilfully discarded decades before. Today, at Guy's Cancer-Free Centre, it came to me finely wrapped in the person of the Chaplain, Mia Holborn.

She reminded me that the first thing humans did after being created was to rest.* The biblical day begins with sundown ('So the evening and the morning were the sixth day'). The biblical day begins with rest. She encouraged me to rest. Jesus also encourages us to rest. In Matthew's gospel He instructs us to learn from Him, 'For I am meek and lowly in heart and you will find rest for your souls.'† I discovered that getting adequate rest made it easier to repent. It was a key to having that 'clean heart' I had been hearing about, so that I could once again be saved. This time, from the lie called cancer.

The uplift from the chaplain's visit remained as I settled in for my long day in the chair. Lurch and I put on the miles while several litres of fluid filtered their way through my system. In between gadabouts, I nodded off for an hour or so at a time. As I did this – dropping in and out of sleep through the day – I had a growing realisation of my true situation. I had no control over it, couldn't guide it, and possessed no management of it. I was not the master of my own destiny. As this dawned on me, the horizon over which that revelation rose revealed its answer. I had a choice: approach whatever was to come as a problem, or as an opportunity.

---

* Study the timeline in Genesis 1:27 – 2:3.

† Matthew 11:29. See also Jeremiah 6:16.

Problems must be solved, but that leads to doing things under my own power. Opportunities must be seized, and I need God's help for that. Let me explain. I'm completely weak when it comes to solving a problem like cancer. I have no power there. But, if I can *surrender* to what is happening, and let it be God's problem, then my only need is to listen for His directives and watch for His signs.

I had been doing that superficially until the third round of chemotherapy, when I fell into my Dark Night. Where had I gone wrong? The answer finally became obvious, and it came because of the Eucharist celebration. Humbling myself at the communion table was a needed reminder that I myself am really nothing. I come there with nothing. But, by humbling myself, by truly surrendering, I place myself in God's hands. When I can do that, by the time I leave the communion table, I have everything I need.

Where things had gone terribly wrong for me was in my insistence that I would *not*, *not*, **not** have surgery. I now accepted that it was still possible that surgery might be absolutely necessary to save my life. I surrendered to it. By the time I said 'see you next week' to Lurch, and headed down through the Welcome Village it was clear. It was all too clear. I was back at the beginning. If surgery was what it took, then surgery was what it took.

In writer Jan Karon's 'Mitford' novels, she has her characters pray 'the prayer that never fails.' It was time for me to follow suit: *'Your will be done.'* After all, if that prayer worked for Jesus in the Garden of Gethsemane, it would undoubtedly work for me.

---

17 September, 2019

Acceptance achieved, decision made, we found enough grace to get through each day. God continued to give us our daily bread, spiritual as well as physical, and we were confident of always remaining in His care. The apostle Paul talked about that daily grace, also in the light of his own insufficiency. He wrote the Corinthian church about how the Lord told him, "My grace is sufficient for you, for My strength is made perfect in weakness."* That was a perfect description of my life. I had nothing but weakness now. I had moved completely to the cliff's edge, and was now steeling myself to jump.

---

23 September, 2019

Round Four, Day Eight. This is truly my last day in chemotherapy, and in a way I'll miss Lurch. I've spent no little time speaking with him in my mind. Rather like Wilson in 'Castaway,' he long ago became Friday to my Crusoe. Reverend Joshua came through again, providing encouragement and prayer. He understood what I meant by standing on the edge of the cliff. 'Don't worry,' he said. 'Jesus will hold your hand, right after Holy Spirit pushes you!' His wide smile lit up the room. 'And then the Father will catch you!'

It was like a switch had been flipped. A month ago the only term to describe my state of being was 'hell.' And, although I was certainly not in heaven, I thought I could see it from here. It was all a result of surrender. I had surrendered to the truth.

* 2 Corinthians 12:9 (for greater context, you might want to study from verse 7 through verse 12), also Romans 5:3-5

Every time something at the Cancer-Free Centre is disinfected, workers put a green sticker on it that announces I AM CLEAN. When I arrived this morning, the sticker showed that my chair had been sanitised the previous Friday. I peeled it off and stuck it in my journal. It was a prophetic act of faith. I did it for me. I did it for Tony, still proclaiming L I F E as he bent his bow. I am clean! Clean from cancer. I left with a spring in my step and a sparkle in my life that I hadn't had in some months.

For the fourth time, I'd expected to play the same old game. Two weeks like this: Five days up from the steroids, two days of diarrhoea and exhaustion, then a week of rest and recovery. But this cycle it was very, very different. Something had shifted since my surrender. The high wasn't as high, the low barely low at all. I became stronger as the cycle continued, not weaker. Instead of being worn down and crushed by chemotherapy, I was refreshed and refilled, against all predictions.

This was notwithstanding the fact I was up at least four times each night to pee. I carried a lot of physical fatigue, but it didn't matter. I continued to be encouraged in dreams, refreshed and refilled. Two days before this I'd begun to sniffle and sneeze, but I fought it; I rejected it. I refused to put my arms out to 'catch' it, and today, it had run its course.

Side effects? Weakness? Pah! I am strong. Compromised immune system? Pah! I am clean.

---

10 October, 2019

Dear Friends,

Thank you all once again for being faithful and loyal prayer partners during these past three months of chemotherapy. I've had my final scans and we'll review them Friday with recommendations for further treatment, either radiotherapy or surgery to remove my bladder. We're in the Father's hands and are at peace with the knowledge that He will speak to us through the doctors. So whatever they say, we will do.

We know that whatever happens, God's grace will draw us both closer to Him. God has already given us many gifts during this time, including the gift of you all! And we are most grateful.

*'Rejoice always. Pray without ceasing. In everything give thanks, for this is the will of God in Christ Jesus concerning you.'**

---

11 October, 2019

I had jumped off the cliff, and had been safely caught. I was ready to do what was called for. Melanie and I were ushered into the consultation room, where Dr. Brio turned to us, smiling, from his computer monitor. After the obligatory small

* 1 Thessalonians 5:16

talk, including another comment on how well I appeared, he turned the monitor toward us and pointed at the image.

'Your tumour really didn't shrink much during the additional chemo,' he said. 'I know you wanted to avoid surgery if you could.'

Melanie and I looked at one another. 'Here it comes,' we both thought.

Brio stunned us by saying, 'Radiotherapy is still on the table.' Our blank faces and extended silence caused him to repeat himself. 'You're still a candidate for radiotherapy,' he said.

We were both shocked. Our understanding from the previous visit was that unless the tumour was gone or almost gone, I'd certainly go under the knife. The doctor continued with his usual enthusiasm. 'Sometimes people with tumours that don't respond all that well to chemo will respond to radio. So with your permission, we'd like to proceed in that fashion.'

'Yes, yes, a thousand times YES!' I shouted inside. In my heart I was dancing on the ceiling with joy and thanksgiving. 'Thank God. Of course,' I managed to stutter.

Who knows what goes through doctors' minds? I certainly don't. What they reveal (exclusively or not) or withhold from me has always been a mystery. Brio is no different. He isn't playing God, but is unknowingly standing in for Him today. All along he's told me only what I actually needed to know to make it to the next step. I'm thankful for his steadiness, encouragement and expertise.

He went on to explain that I'll have still more scans and tests and begin radiotherapy in November. After a six or seven week cycle, I'd be scanned again in the spring.

I agreed to participate in a trial for an improved method of radiotherapy treatment. It's called **RAIDER**, which stands for **R**andomised phase II trial of **A**daptive **I**mage guided standard or **D**ose **E**scalated tumour boost **R**adiotherapy in the treatment of transitional cell carcinoma of the bladder. Someone worked really hard to nail that acronym. The logo was pretty cute too. The letter 'I' in RAIDER was like the stem of a balloon that was obviously drawn to be a bladder. It had a little spot in it, representing the tumour. The stem of the balloon was, of course, the 'water works.'

After filling out the paperwork and agreeing to take part in the trial, we headed home, humbled but happy. This all turned out how we had hoped, but not how we had expected. Yes, we had prayed, and petitioned God for complete healing through divine means, and barring that, radiotherapy instead of life-altering surgery. All the prophetic signs pointed to it, over and over again. And yet, when crunch time came, I had to surrender completely to the thing I feared, what I once thought of as 'the horrors of surgery'.

Somehow, God had made surgery all right to contemplate. 'My grace is sufficient for you,' He had said, over and over. I'd finally gotten the message. My joy was tempered by an overwhelming sense of being humbled by good fortune. We sent a message to our Faithful Pray-ers:

Our prayer needs now are simple: we pray for our outlook, not for an outcome (Romans 8:31). Outcome is clearly in God's hands and we are confident He will provide grace for whatever we need, which He knows best (Ephesians 3:20).

We also pray for presence, not process (Romans 8:7). If we have His presence, the process is His and we don't manage it (Proverbs 3:5-6). We pray to the Healer and give thanks in His mighty name (1 Chronicles 16:11).

May we continue to walk with increasing humility during this season (Ephesians 4:1-3)! Thank you all for your prayers. In helping us carry our burden, you fulfil the law of Christ (Galatians 6:2).

---

25 October, 2019

Life came more back to normal as the clock ticked down to the beginning of radiotherapy in November. I continued to walk as much as possible, to keep my leg strength, as well as for the cardio value. Melanie and I had taken a long stroll the previous weekend – about seven miles along part of London's Green Chain and Thames Path. As the week progressed, my left ankle began aching, probably from too much pavement-pounding, I thought. I was changing into bedclothes and did a double-take as I saw my legs.

My left calf was visibly much larger than my right. I had been warned about Deep Vein Thrombosis (DVT). The swelling could be from a blood clot. We measured it, poked at it. Yup, the leg was definitely swollen. It's not unusual for cancer patients to develop a blood clot in the larger muscles. If one breaks free and migrates to the lung, it can block the blood supply. Such a pulmonary embolism kills often enough, so I took it very seriously.

It was pushing 10:00 p.m. on a Friday night and suddenly we were back out of our pyjamas, dressing for a trip to Accident & Emergency (A & E), where the unfortunate are met by the compassionate. Wheeling north to see my old friends at Kings College Hospital, Melanie thought she'd have to drop me off. Even at this time of night, Denmark Hill is a busy four-lane road, and there are fewer than a half-dozen parking spaces on the street near the hospital.

Amazingly, as we rolled past Ruskin Park, there on the left was a parking space, right outside the entrance to A&E! Melanie did a quick parallel park into the tiny space,* and as I got out of the car, I broke into laughter and couldn't stop. After securing the car and pushing in the wing mirror, Melanie

* All London parking spaces are tiny. Good luck with that double-cab pickup truck, Bubba.

joined me to catch the joke. The SUV in front of us sported a sticker in the rear window. It reminded us that GOD IS HERE.

I was still chuckling as we walked into A&E to register. For a Friday, it was a quiet night. No trauma cases. No one with bloody bandages. No screamers. No drunks. Nothing violent was going on. No one was arguing. What I grew up with on American television did not prepare me for this. It was more like waiting for a haircut than being triaged for emergency service. Within ten minutes, we faced a calm and pleasant nurse practitioner, who told us I'd normally be sent for an ultrasound, but it was now closed until Monday.

Instead, he took blood. 'I'll have the lab do what's called a D-dimer test. It tells whether there are pieces of clot floating around in your blood. There's a threshold number, and if you're below the number, you're okay.'

'What if I'm above the number?'

'Well then we give you an anti-coagulant to take until Monday, when you can come in and have the ultrasound.'

A half hour later, the results were back. 'You're right on the borderline, so to be on the safe side, we'll send you home with two doses of heparin to take at bedtime tomorrow and Sunday.' He turned and reached for an item on his desk. I expected to have pills passed into my hand, not syringes.

'These are self-injectors – you can't mess them up and you can't stick yourself. Here – I'll show you how to use them while you have the first dose.'

It was a pretty amazing device, actually. Some genius figured out that you could put a full syringe inside a plastic sleeve and spring-load it two ways. The NP uncapped the device but this didn't (exclusively) reveal the needle – that was still down in its plastic collar. He handed it to Melanie.

She pinched up a roll of my abdomen and placed the plastic collar against it. *POP goes the weasel,* and the needle dove hungrily into my flesh. So far, so good. Then the plunger was pushed. Oh, oh, oh! The serum had the viscosity of honey, and as it s l o w l y forced its way into the muscle, it created an expanding sphere of pain. Within 20 seconds I felt as though I'd been doing 10 times as many crunches as were good for me. Once home, I curled up into the foetal position to protect myself, and considered whether I'd ever move again.

---

28 October, 2019

I'm now completely over heparin, and never want to ride the Inject-O-Rama ever again. I retained a small seed of hope that it would be possible to straighten up again someday without intense abdominal pain. Now that it was Monday, the DVT clinic at Kings was open.

Date: 28/10/19

No Evidence of a Clinically Significant Deep Vein Thrombosis (DVT)

Leg L - DVT Duplexl - Vasc
US Compression venography lower limb Lt.

SITE	LEFT
External iliac:	No Thrombus
Common femoral:	No Thrombus
Profunda femoris:	No Thrombus
Femoral:	No Thrombus
Popliteal:	No Thrombus
Gastrocnemius:	No Thrombus
Soleal vein:	No Thrombus
Posterior tibial:	No Thrombus
Anterior tibial:	No Thrombus
Peroneal vein:	No Thrombus
Long sapheneous:	No Thrombus
Short sapheneous:	No Thrombus

Summary — No DVT

Comments: — No evidence of DVT in the left leg.

---

30 October, 2019

And that should have been that. Only it wasn't. The morning after the ultrasound, I was again passing blood. That was not good. There wasn't any pain involved, and I'd almost been cured of the automatic thought: *'I wonder what's going to come out this time?'* That was yesterday, and it was bad enough. Today it was worse. Today it was clotted blood.

I'd quickly concluded this might be related to the heparin injections. If my surgical wound was still not fully healed, I surmised the anti-coagulant could ~~cause me to bleed out entirely~~ be a disadvantage. The smart course was to head to the Urology Centre as a walk-in patient, so I did, producing a urine sample, then waiting my turn. I should have packed a lunch. The standing-room-only crowd took more than four hours to clear. Early in the afternoon, I was finally seen by an upbeat young physician about the age of my granddaughter. I was duly interviewed, history was taken and my sample results were reviewed.

She asked, 'Did you know you have blood in your urine?'

'No. What a complete surprise!'

It wasn't really like that. She was actually pushing 30, and like everyone else I had worked with, was very competent and professional. She agreed that my current condition *may* be related to the heparin, and told me to go home and keep an eye on things. If I didn't get better, she said, I was free to return to the clinic any weekday.

---

31 October, 2019

I awoke early in the morning with a serious need to empty my bladder and trundled across the hallway to stand in front of the toilet, ready.

And I stood.

And I stood.

Nothing happened. I mean I knew I *wanted* to go, I *needed* to go, and my bladder was *trying*, but it was failing. I sensed that something was blocking the water works, and I knew just what it was. *'Oh crap. I need to be catheterised,'* I thought. I checked the time: 6.45 a.m. I needed the Urology clinic, not A & E, but had a long way to go (no pun intended). The clinic didn't open until nine. Melanie left for work about eight. After she did, I struggled back to stand in front of the toilet.

And I stood.

And I stood.

I was afraid to 'push.' After all, I wasn't about to deliver a baby. In truth, I had no idea what I was doing. I only knew what I was *not* doing. Passing a clot, even a relatively large one, had never been painful at all. I merely had the sensation of a soft lump moving through the system. Now I had pain from pressure, and a sensation that a door had been slammed shut.

The urge to pee left once again and I retreated, getting ready to catch a train that would get me in clinic as close to 9.00 a.m. as possible. Just as I was ready to head out the door the urge returned. Better safe than sorry, I thought. Once again I assumed the position. This time, there was pain to go with the pressure, and it built and built until it had me leaning against the wall to steady myself. I was about to consider sitting down when the dam broke.

It was like delivering a loaf of bread, and it left me with a metallic taste in my mouth. Now perspiring, but greatly relieved, I walked to the corner, had perfect timing to catch the bus, which delivered me with perfect timing to catch the train. My Transport for London chauffeurs were on the ball.

Back in the clinic I again lacked a reservation and so waited again for a table. At least I was prepared for a siege, with a full backpack. Today's exceedingly youthful clinic specialist was male instead of female, but it didn't matter. Their interest in me and their eagerness to serve was interchangeable. I was quickly subjected to a catheter for lavage and the wash water came out almost clear. This was very good news. Whatever was bleeding had apparently mostly stopped. I had no obvious urinary symptoms otherwise and no pyrexia or haemodynamic instability.

Pyrexia means fever. Haemodynamic stability means I have a healthy blood pressure. Not sure why they just can't write 'No fever' and 'Bloody good BP' on the report. Probably the same reason half of it is literally Greek to me. After all the manhandling, I'm ready to head home, but was told to wait a while. I'm not overly compliant by nature, but I know better than to simply wander off while burdened with their catheter. I'd forgotten my slide whistle in any case.

After another hour, Dr. Cub Scout returned to announce they would keep me in hospital overnight for observation. Just a precaution, he said. I texted Melanie the details and off I went to the Aston Key Urology ward. The male portion of the ward has 17 beds. I'm in number 14.

This was not like an American hospital. The beds were partitioned by fabric, not walls. Remove the signature NHS Blue fanfold screens and it would look like we're on location in a World War II military hospital ward. Aston Key is on the fourth floor, and the pigeon-flecked window provided a stunning view of nearby rooftops and a moribund HVAC stack.

However, it was very clean and ship-shape inside, and I checked in with dispatch. They even gifted me with free red grippy-slippers that clashed horribly with my backless gown. Oh well, Fashionista beggars can't be choosers, even with a £134 billion budget available. Melanie stopped by later with some essentials and stayed a while after my dinner. I might have let her beat me in a game of cards.

About 7:30 I got a new neighbour. Laszlo was, by the sounds of it, also an American, and his chatterbox companion was clearly French. They had a loud continuous awkwardly intimate conversation two metres away, either not realising or not caring that the screen only blocked sight, not sound. 'Nitter natter.' 'Ha ha ha.' 'Chitter chatter,' 'Tee hee hee.'

Meanwhile, the man across the way in Bed 17 tried vainly and repeatedly to carry on a phone conversation, but the call kept dropping. 'Allo? Huh? Huh?' he would shout loudly. He would then mumble menacingly in a strange guttural language, followed by a brief reconnect. 'You hear now? Good. Bla bla bla...Allo? Huh? Huh?'

'Nitter natter.' 'You hear now?' 'Ha ha ha.' 'You hear now? Good.' 'Chitter chatter,' 'Bla bla bla...Allo? Huh? Huh?' 'Tee hee hee.' That was the agonising soundtrack at Aston Key that Halloween, and it continued well past the end of visiting hours at 8:30. My imagination can create more gruesome scenarios, but few more annoying. Finally, around 10:00, the frequent caller finally gave up and Laszlo's sweetheart swept off the floor like a ship under sail.

It had been a long day and my catheter showed I was still bleeding a little, but things were improving there. There was hope for the future. The ward lights were finally dimmed about 10:30. I somehow managed to drift off to sleep, exhausted. There was one consolation. I'm grateful that, although I snore profusely, it never wakes me and neither does anything else. To Laszlo, and the man in Bed 17, my glottis spent the night asking, 'Allo? You hear now?'

---

1 November, 2019

I awoke early, not because anything was happening, but from long habit. There was no need to get up and take a leak so I'd slept for more than six hours. The previous day's exhaustion was gone. It was still dark outside and the ward lights remained dimmed. I hefted my two-plus pounds of catheter bag ('a pint a pound the world around'*) and shuffled down the corridor to the toilet. It was like carrying a football downfield in very, very slow motion.

Other patients were in various forms of sleep in various poses at various levels of undress as I passed. I nodded at the night nurse (now the exhausted early morning nurse), who glanced my way briefly and returned to his paperwork. Business concluded, back at Bed 14, I did my usual morning routine. I made the bed, fluffed the pillow, changed my shorts and shirt, washed up a bit (I had my own sink!), straightened the materials on my side-table, and then settled in under my prayer shawl to read. I had less than two minutes of peace.

Laszlo began crying bloody murder. He apparently pushed the call button all of 10 nanoseconds prior, and when the ward nurse didn't come sprinting, he began yelling. It woke everyone else, and certainly gained my attention. 'I need help! Help me! It burns! It burns,' he shrieked, just like Gollum complaining about being tied up with the elf rope. Working through my seventh month of urinary pain, I thought at first he was overwrought. *'Does this guy have no pain threshold?'*

But as the noise level and the frequency of the complaint both increased I exchanged judgment for mercy, and actually became concerned. It was his catheter. Normally, they don't hurt internally, they just cause irritation where the tube leaves the body, or if it gets banged around a bit (the author said, speaking as a worldly and grizzled veteran of two full catheterisations).

The problem was beyond the nurse, so she called in the matron. The screaming continued during the next examination, so the urologist on call was bleeped. Five minutes later he treated us all to a thoroughly excruciating exchange through

* A pint of urine actually weighs 1.04 pounds, except Imperial pints, which are a pound and a quarter.

the privacy screen. I was blind to everything happening in the next bed of course, but my over-active imagination provided a vivid idea of the gruesome scene six feet away.

The doctor began his assessment: 'Let's find out what the problem is?' Laszlo whimpered in response and swallowed a shriek.

'All right, let's find the source of that pain. How about this, does this hurt?' There was no swallowing of this shriek, nor the yell, or the cursing that followed. I thought back to Baby's First Cystoscopy and shuddered sympathetically, glancing around fearfully for Angel #2.

The doctor continued his relentless probing. 'I see,' he said unemotionally. 'How about this?' Laszlo then imitated Nigel Tufnel's amplifier in This is Spinal Tap. His volume went up to eleven. Melanie had thoughtfully brought a pair of earplugs for me the previous night. They were of no use. Military grade noise-cancelling headphones wouldn't have worked. I was left praying for the poor fellow.

It turned out that his catheter had been inserted *too far* and was actually poking into the top of his bladder. Yowch! The urologist ordered some saline, inflated Laszlo's bladder with it, inducing still more screaming, deflated the balloon (more screaming), made an adjustment (more screaming) and then beat a hasty retreat, awaiting his next bleep into someone else's crisis.

As this drama wound down, my breakfast arrived. 'Ah!,' I thought. 'I can enjoy this in peace.' But it was not to be. Just then, Laszlo's lady friend was back. Because she missed the show, she (and I) got to relive it again in painful detail, even through my earplugs. I remained thankful for free health care, but at that moment I would have shelled out £1000 per day for a private room. Not because of the screaming, but the treacle-ish love-fest. If they didn't quit soon, I thought, I'd have to be transferred to the diabetic ward.

I survived it all, and was released from the hospital mid-afternoon, after being 'successfully TWOC'd.' TWOC means 'Trial Without Catheter,' which sounds suspiciously like a Star Chamber event. In actuality, it simply meant I was competent to pee without help, the dream of every urology patient.

---

6 November, 2019

About a week later I awoke earlier than usual and headed into my study. Opening the Bible, I flipped idly through the Gospel of John until my attention was drawn to the resurrection of Lazarus in chapter 11. You might remember that Lazarus was a friend of Jesus, and he had died unexpectedly.

Jesus arrived in Bethany several days after Lazarus was put in the tomb. He ordered the tomb opened, and then turned his attention to heaven. Then Jesus said, 'Father, thank you for hearing Me. You always hear Me, but I said it out loud for the sake of all these people standing here, so that they will believe you sent me.'*

Then Jesus summoned Lazarus out of the tomb, and he lived again. That's me, I thought. I *am* Lazarus, originally pulled out of the grave when I was born again years ago. Now, I was being pulled out of the grave of death-by-cancer. This idea of being Lazarus – saved from what others around me are seeing as 'certain death' remained vividly in my mind during a noontime meet-up with Melanie, and one of her friends, Afusat.

Afusat was there because she'd had a burden to pray for me, and she did, with a passion. She quoted James 5, and Psalms 91 and 25 ('Watch over my life, and deliver me!'). Then,

---

* John 11:41-42 (NLT)

she began making declarations from the latter part of John 11. 'You will rise like Lazarus! You will not rest in the grave! You will be strong and healthy!' The 'coincidence' of it made me weak in the knees. 'Glory to God!' is all Afusat could say when I told her about it.

It was the first Wednesday of the month, which meant our church's regular prayer meeting. We settled in, and quieted ourselves for the opening prayer. The Reverend Tim Jones began by reading John 11:38-44, about the resurrection of Lazarus. I laughed out loud. I couldn't help myself.

---

15 November, 2019

November was a nice break after the rigours of chemotherapy. Since that fourth round had begun, and I came out of my Dark Night, I was increasingly strong. Melanie joined me for another check-in with Brio, which was to be followed by the installation of a PICC line. PICC stands for Peripherally Inserted Central Catheter. After having yet another needle shoved into my arm *('Sharp scratch!')*, a slim catheter would be inserted through a vein, past the shoulder and then down into my chest cavity within the superior vena cava, ending somewhere just north-west of my right atrium.

It had taken a while for me to realise that 'radiotherapy' is actually 'chemo-radiotherapy.' Yup, I had the pleasure of still more chemo, this time from a portable box attached to the PICC. *'Thank you, waiter. I'll have the freshly generated X-rays with a side-dish of toxins please!'* For the first week of my radiotherapy, and again for the third week, I would carry a small pump (let's continue the Addams Family theme and call it Thing) full of chemotherapy drug. Tik, tik, tik. Drip, drip, drip. Life, life, life.

I wasn't excited about hauling Thing around for a week at a time, nor about having a half-metre of polyurethane stuffed obtrusively into my body for an extended stay.* But I accepted it. How often in my treatment, when I became used to an idea did things change?

'I've got bad news and good news,' the irrepressible Dr. Brio exclaimed that morning. Before I even interjected something as mundane as 'Oh?' he continued. 'The drug we're supposed to use for the RAIDER trial, mitomycin, isn't available. There's a worldwide shortage. There's only one manufacturer and the last batch they turned out didn't pass inspection.'

He paused, just in case I wanted to say something meaningful like, 'Oh?' and then plowed ahead. 'Since we can't use that particular drug, it means we can't use the slow-drip pump, which means you won't be getting a PICC line today!' Mental high-fives all around. So what *did* it mean?

It meant a return to Cisplatin, 'which we already know you tolerate well,' the doctor added. 'I personally think it works better than the mitomycin, so I'm happy about that!' When the doctor's happy, everybody's happy, I guess. My unexpected weekly reunion with Lurch would recommence Monday morning. Radiotherapy would begin Monday afternoon.

Speaking of which, I'll toss in an oddity here. My original radiotherapy schedule was supposed to stretch into January. But for no reason that anyone at NHS could account for, my schedule was changed, and I'd be done with my treatment on 31 December.

Those of us who live in a prophetic state of mind keep our eyes open for circumstances, objects and actions that draw our attention. They could be God speaking to us.† This calendar change stood out as one of those things. The new year, and the

* My advice is to look for an extended stay option. Renting a PICC line by the month is always cheaper.

† We test them of course. See footnote in entry from 30 July, 2019

new decade, would begin with a clean slate, and a fresh vision. 'You will spring to new life', I thought.

On the way out, Brio assured me, with a chuckle, that I'd soon find out why radiotherapy to the pelvic region is known to oncologists as 'the world's most expensive laxative.' Thank God my haemorrhoids had been healed years ago.

---

18 November, 2019 (morning)

'Hello again, Lurch'

'______'

He glanced down at me with his usual disdain. His thought balloon was readable. 'Back for more trips to the loo, are we? Can't manage anything more exciting than that?' What an insufferable prat he was. I didn't dignify his comments with a response. I was already looking around the suite for Reverend Joshua. He'd been on my mind when I first awakened, and I'd planned to send him a note at his office. As Lurch and I came out of the toilet for the third time that morning, there he was.

His beaming face greeted me as he came to sit. 'It's so good to see you again. You told me you were done with the chemotherapy,' he said.

I explained how the ruined mitomycin forced the last-minute change of plan. Not having a PICC line had returned me to my little hut in the Chemotherapy Village. He paused and then asked me, 'Remember what's written in Romans Eight? "We know that all things work together for good to those who love God, to those who are called according to His purpose,"' he quoted. 'The Lord has turned this tragedy into a good thing for you.'

As he rose to leave, Joshua said, 'You noticed I was surprised to see you? It wasn't so much because I thought you were done with the chemotherapy chair. It was because I didn't intend to visit this ward at all today. I was going to work exclusively upstairs. But the Spirit prompted me to come here.'

All things work together for good. I sat back in the chair and stared out the window at the chilly jumble of clouds running before the light northerly wind. It was six months to the day since the crime showed up in that South London urinal. Many of the days along the way had been difficult, but I was reminded that 'tribulation produces patience, patience produces character, and character produces hope.' More wisdom from Paul's letter to the Romans. It ends with the good news that I get to share my hope with others.

It's an amazing thing when the truth of scripture unfolds in my own life, right before my eyes. There have been (and still are) many hard and flinty places inside me. But God's grace is like water. Given enough time, it wears away the rough edges, and makes them smooth, like a pebble on a beach. Tik, tik, tik. Drip, drip, drip. Life, life, life.

---

18 November, 2019 (afternoon)

Immediately after chemo I took the lift downstairs to the Radiotherapy Village. The lobby is large and sprawling, and both wings of it have rows of doors leading to dressing rooms. 1-6 give entry to three of the six radiotherapy suites, 7-12 to the other.

There was no waiting for my first session of radiotherapy, because they wanted to ~~nuke me~~ provide treatment the very minute I was done with the Cisplatin drip and on saline for post-treatment hydration. More than a few people did a double-take at Lurch, especially in the lift, which can be full of visitors and neophytes. Some backed away without realising it.

As soon as I arrived, the Radiotherapy receptionist picked up the phone and I was escorted directly back. It was like being on the A list at The Ritz. Well, not quite. I was met in the back by Helen, who was one of my main minders for the six and a half weeks of treatments.

'Have you voided your bladder?' she asked. I nodded in the affirmative.

'Go do it again to make sure.' I sulkily complied, thinking ignobly, 'What does she know?'

A lot, as it turned out. The previous Friday, the day I was supposed to have my PICC installed, was actually my first day on the radiotherapy bed. But it wasn't to receive an X-ray dose. No, it was for Baby's First Tattoo. Yes, I can exclusively reveal that I am one of the 89 Americans under 70 who have yet to get at least one tattoo. That day, I got three: one on my lower abdomen directly over the centre of my bladder, and one on each hip. Each was the size of a pen-point, about a half-millimetre around.

I lay in my gown, shorts lowered just to the point where they might possibly have pretended to provide modesty. The technicians turned on the guide lasers (more about those later) and adjusted the height of the bed: up down; up-down; back-forth; there – just right. They adjusted the foot of the bed for my height. They adjusted the movable hump that sat behind my knees.

They were lining me up against the reference scan that had been taken back on 7 November. That was a detailed MRI picture of where everything lay inside of me. After all, it was important that what's left of the tumour sit precisely in the ~~blast zone~~ window of treatment. When I had been lined up to their satisfaction, they marked the three points with dye and poked each set in quickly with a needle. I was disappointed that no one said, 'Sharp scratch!'

19 November, 2019

I was still hanging out at the Healing Rooms most Tuesdays, but now as a client, not as a volunteer. I received prayer, which also provided encouragement. I personally know of people supernaturally healed of cancer. I've heard them speak and seen their inexplicable medical reports. What God has done, he could do again. This is why we pray for healing. This is why we share healing testimony. It's also why I have faith for healing.

This particular day I was seated with a man who's a friend of mine, and two women I didn't know well. Voldemar knew the specifics of my medical condition, the women did not. The three of them laid hands on me and let Holy Spirit speak to them. Voldemar saw a word over my head – *'CELEBRATE!'* he roared. 'This is what the Lord is telling you now: Celebrate! He has good things coming your way.'

Lori said 'I hear the Lord saying Luke 7:4. I can't quote it…' And so I pulled open my Bible and read, 'When they came to Jesus, they asked Him earnestly, saying, "You should do this for him for he is worthy."' The passage related to a healing story – the story of the Centurion's servant.

Finally, Faith said 'I'm also getting a picture. I don't understand it, but maybe it will mean something to you. I see a tube, more like a pipe, and there are bits coming out of it and landing at the foot of the Cross.' Huh. Just like the bit of scab that appeared later that afternoon.

21 November, 2019

I was now travelling each weekday to the Cancer-Free Centre, ~~being zapped~~ receiving treatment five days a week for 32 sessions. It was nothing less than commuting to a job with no pay. I appreciated the routine, and regular walking to and from the train station, because my body continued to fall out of shape. Before all this began, I had been working out and running regularly. My time for 1,500 metres had been just over eight minutes. Now, although I had the strength to run, there was no stamina to keep up the pace. My veins were tired and couldn't move oxygen fast enough.

One feature of my radiotherapy was a weekly meeting with the RAIDER team. I had a height and weight check and then answered questions about my condition (with a great emphasis on waste elimination). My weekly meetings were with a lovely Tamil physician named Girvan. At the end of our first interview, during the small talk, I told him about my recent run from the Cancer-Free Centre to the train platform at London Bridge Station.

After radiotherapy two days before, there were only five minutes until the next train. So, I pushed through the front doors of the Cancer-Free Centre and began to run. It's more than 500 metres past the hospital, across St. Thomas Street and up the escalator to London Bridge Station. I sprinted all the way to the top. My pulse was back to normal by the time I reached the end of Platform 13. He somehow misunderstood the story as a question.

'No, Mr. Searle, you cannot claim that sprinting to catch a train is an absence of side-effect.' Like everyone else, Girvan assured me that I'll undoubtedly grow weaker and weaker for many weeks, even after radiotherapy is complete. I refused to believe him. We'll see.

Today was session four in the tanning booth, 10 minutes of technical fiddling for 90 seconds of ionising radiation. The dose is measured in Grays (Gy), two Gy per session. A Gray measures dosage and is equivalent to a millisievert (mSv), the function used to measure exposure as a hazard. 1 Gy = 1 mSv. The UK average annual dose per person is about 2.7 mSv. A CT scan might give out 1.5 mSv. According to Public Health England, it would take 1,000 mSv in a month to make me really sick. 5,000 in a month is a 50% chance of death.*

I'll only receive 64 Gy in all, well below any level of harm. Probably. Before treatment began I signed a consent form agreeing I'd been told that in some cases, radiotherapy itself can cause cancer. Oh well, so can bacon,† and you'll have to pry *that* from my cold, dead fingers.

On days when there's no press of time due to chemotherapy, I signed in at Radiotherapy reception and waited for a page, sometimes up to an hour, depending on what was happening backstage. The Cancer-Free Centre's paging system is brilliant and efficient. Large computer-driven reader boards are scattered around the Villages having the largest daily cattle call, like Welcome and Radiotherapy. This is how the Cancer-Free Centre manages those 4,000 visitors a day.

Patient names appear with instructions or destinations. You might see CLARK, William --- Blood Draw, or SEARLE, Alan --- G3 Carnation. That was my destination most days, the third of the six suites, each one named after a flower: Aster, Buttercup, Carnation, and so on.‡

When the board showed my name, I'd move into a vacant changing room, remembering to lock the doors on both sides. After disrobing to my shorts, t-shirt and socks, I'd stuff my

* https://www.gov.uk/government/publications/ionising-radiation-dose-comparisons/ionising-radiation-dose-comparisons (accessed 10 April, 2020)

† https://www.cancer.org/healthy/eat-healthy-get-active/acs-guidelines-nutrition-physical-activity-cancer-prevention/food-additives.html (accessed 10 April, 2020)

‡ The best patient name of all during my weeks there was ATTA-BOYE, John. I don't know you friend, but felicitations to your parents for choosing to hyphenate your name. 'John Atta-Boye' is much more distinctive than 'John Boye'. Ask the Waltons.

worldly goods into a small plastic basket, like a shopping basket. Then, making sure my NHS high-fashion gown was tied well enough to keep me modest (such as it is with any backless hospital gown) I stepped into the curved back corridor running the length of the building.

There's a sign for G3 Carnation with a chair set beneath it, where I would park myself. Eventually, the massive shielded door to the radiotherapy suite would quietly grind open. I anticipated Helen's trademark directive then, cycling myself through the toilet one more time. Then I would enter the suite, set down my basket and lie on the clear plastic bed. I hunched my tightey-whiteys down *just far enough* that the techs (they are almost all female) can drape paper towel over anything exposed. Unsurprisingly, these ladies are all extremely proficient at keeping eye contact.

Part of the daily ritual was to repeat my full name, date of birth *and* street address (postal code not sufficient). Y'know, just in case matching my face to the picture on my file wasn't enough, Or in case there was an Alan Searle doppelgänger with my birth date cycling through radiotherapy just then.

The bed is part of a truck-sized device called a linear accelerator, or Linac machine. The business portion is shaped like a giant handset from a 1950s desk telephone. As the bed slides back underneath this, it crouches over the bed like a cur dog over its bowl. Someone has thoughtfully put a small yellow smiley-face sticker next to the output window, which made me laugh.

The machine is calibrated along two axes that are marked by green laser light crossing the room at right angles horizontally. These allow the techs to line me up exactly on the bed. X marks the spot, as it were. The laser lights are a more sophisticated version of laser levels used in the construction trades, and they meet one another across the ceiling over the bed, where a plus sign is cut out of the drop-ceiling panel for reference.

This cut-out is directly in my line of vision as I lie still for treatment. It took me a few sessions to realise that it mimics the cross of Christ.

---

25 November, 2019

When I awoke the previous Saturday after a week of ~~phaser fire~~ radiotherapy, my bladder was sore. I was certain it was *the very specific target, the centre of the issue.* That's where the pain was centred. Girvan told me later that some patients experience that, but he wasn't convinced it wasn't psychosomatic.

Whatever. All I knew was that this was a different type of pain. It was a deep ache. It wasn't severe, but it was persistent. It was an I-Don't-Feel-Like-I-Want-To-Feel level pain. But by today, a Monday, it had receded again and I was back for another round.

Melanie had started our day by putting on a worship music set from YouTube. The pastor's introduction quoted the first five verses of Psalm 42, which beg the Lord for revival. I tried hard not to become fixated on the line, 'My enemies mock me over and over, saying "Where is this God of yours: Why doesn't he help you?"'*

It's another long day at the Cancer-Free Centre, first with Lurch and then in the tanning booth. Mondays are a big tug of

* Psalm 42:3 (TPT)

war between the chemo nurses and the radio techs. The chemo nurses always spend several hours filling me as full of liquids as they can manage. The radio techs immediately want me as empty as possible. This had the potential for a compelling television reality show, I thought. No worse than *Toddlers and Tiaras* or the Channel 4 version of *Great British Bake-off*.

Because of Lurch, I didn't have to change clothes, but I was tipped off the previous week about this, and wore workout slacks with an elastic waist. Once again I received the VIP treatment: no waiting.

After the name-birthdate-address doppelgänger-prevention routine, all the lining up was complete. The techs retreated past their curtain and out through the massive protective door. Because I'm limited to staring overhead at the cross of Christ they let me know they're leaving. 'We're leaving now!' or 'See you soon!' they always cried as a courtesy.

'I'll miss you! Hurry back!' I would call in response. They laughed every time. The Linac machine always rotated around me twice. The first time was to scan my bladder to make sure it was lined up properly, and is properly empty, because Helen is always watching. Otherwise, we start over.

During the second rotation, Linac emits a dull continuous beep. That's to let me know that, as the panel outside the protective door says, BEAM ON. The beam itself doesn't make any noise. It's the Linac equivalent of a reversing beeper, an alert about something dangerous. Only it's not dangerous to me.

Psalm 42 continued to rattle through my head all day, especially the doubting bits. '*Why isn't God healing me through all this prayer?*' I echoed the mocking cries of those 'enemies' who asked, 'Where is this God of yours: Why doesn't he help you?' The writer's desire was for God's presence, and he prayed and fasted in hope. One result was this famous line: 'Deep calls to deep, at the noise of your waterfalls; all Your waves and Your billows passed over me.'*

Here's the strange thing. That last verse was on my mind later as I made dinner. I was moved to play worship songs off my phone. It's set to shuffle. The first two songs both used that same verse as their theme. They're the only two songs in my entire music collection, more than 2,100 songs, that do so.

Deep calls to deep, indeed.

---

2 December, 2019

The new month began with my third round of chemotherapy and eleventh session ~~in Helen's microwave cooker~~ on Linac's tanning bed. I checked my body as I stepped out of the shower. The tanning isn't working. My skin is just as dead-fish white as it always was.

I pondered a double dream from overnight. The details were somewhat different in each, but the theme was the same. *I've driven out into a deserted scrub land. It's quiet and remote, and there's no one in sight. I get out and take a walk across huge drifts of glacial moraine. The pebbles slip underfoot and make it difficult to move with confidence. I returned to the car, got in and buckled my belt. Suddenly, someone I don't know is at the window, handing me my keys. Somehow, I'd lost them during my trek.*

I received insight from a friend about these dreams. 'The Lord is reminding you that even in the tough times, the desert times, He holds the keys to your life. He's encouraging you that you still have "places to go."'

---

* Psalm 42:7

After my time in chemotherapy today I went downstairs for the second half of the *'Fill him up!' 'No! Empty him out!'* game being played by my care teams. But this day, I found a surprise waiting for me, my old friend BladderScan last seen back in May. How insulting. *'What? Doesn't Helen trust me to empty myself?'*

It was like driving into a sobriety checkpoint on a Friday night when I haven't been drinking for 15 years: *All right, pull over. Get out of the car. You have the right to refuse this test but you'll automatically go to jail. Yes? All right, lie down and drop trou. Aha! You're over the legal limit!*

Once again, Helen knew best. I'd retained 40 ml, outside the safety zone. I felt vaguely guilty, like a boy literally caught with his pants down. *How did she know?* Too much in the bladder meant ~~they might misfire and render me sterile~~ their aim could be off, so Lurch and I shuffled back to the toilet. I lingered on purpose *(that'll fix her)* and made sure that I emptied myself of

every
last
drop.

---

3 December, 2019

At 4.00 a.m. I lay awake trying to focus on prayer or poetry or something, anything to keep my mind off the stupid lies it wants to tell when my body's at its lowest ebb. It's difficult some nights to stop listening. My ride of faith wasn't over. Most often the train ran smoothly along at a good clip, with a reassuring and relaxing rhythm. Occasionally, I'd pull off deliberately on a side track, waiting for something to pass. Or, my own passage would slow as I bumped over points where one track joined another.

Life then momentarily reeled and floundered side to side and threatened to dump me out like I was derailing. This was one of those times. It was too early to get up, even if I wanted to get up. Those 11 doses of x-rays were beginning to settle in as advertised. The discomfort was constant now.

Melanie shifted in her sleep and suddenly, an invisible hand pressed *hard* on my lower abdomen. All my pain and discomfort vanished immediately, and I slept. When I awoke two hours later I wandered sleepily into my study. My Bible was open on the desk, in the first chapter of the Book of Revelation.

'When I saw him, I fell down at his feet as good as dead, but he laid his right hand on me and I heard his reassuring voice saying, "Don't yield to fear. I am the Beginning and the End, the Living One! I was dead, but now look – I am alive forever and ever. And I hold the keys that unlock death and the unseen world. Now I want you to write what you have seen."'*

---

6 December, 2019

If radiotherapy to the pelvis is truly the world's most expensive laxative, someone's not getting their money's worth. I had no diarrhoea last week, and none this week. It was my personal Red Sea experience. God was holding back the waters. One of my routines for the chemo-radiotherapy, as it was for plain old chemo, was to have blood taken on Fridays. Then the nurses reviewed the results on Monday before they decided whether

* Revelation 1:17-19 (TPT)

I was fit enough to climb in the chair (after I made the cross-town trip to see them, of course).

The blood draw area at the Cancer-Free Centre is always jumping, with more people going in and out than cars at a petrol station. Phlebotomy is old hat to me, as I mentioned, and I whiled away the time searching for a play on words between phlebotomy and lobotomy. It didn't work. This particular Friday I was with Shona, and from the paraphernalia in her cubby I gathered she's from Zimbabwe. She asked the routine question, 'How are you today?' I gave my now-routine answer, 'I'm healed, in Jesus' name.'

She was almost ready to insert the butterfly needle but stopped, looked at me with surprise and said, 'Huh! I don't see many white folks who actually *believe* in Jesus! Sharp scratch!'

---

16 December, 2019

This Monday was chemotherapy infusion number 13, counting back to July. I was also ~~gently roasted~~ received treatment in the Linac for the twenty-first time. At the end of it I was 65% of the way done with radiotherapy. But something odd was happening. I continued to improve, in body and spirit. My blood pressure was taken each Monday before the cannula insertion. It had been deteriorating steadily since July, but was now unexpectedly improving. Before this all began, my BP was typically a healthy 120/60. Last week it had worsened to 160/100.

Today it had bounced back to 138/88. Week on week I began to strengthen. I was more resilient, like something had shifted deep inside me. When I dragged Lurch into the lift for the trip to radiotherapy, I found myself alone there with my consultant. 'Hello! You look fantastic,' Brio offered.

'Thanks,' I replied, 'I feel really good.'

'How many radio sessions have you had now?'

This'll be number twenty-one.'

'You are absolutely the poster child for a positive response to radiotherapy,' he said. And with that, the lift door opened, and he stepped out and went his way.

I believe now that my physical improvement was definitely tied to extended prayer. The Faithful Pray-ers had been concentrating on two verses from my now beloved Isaiah 35, 'Strengthen the weak hands, and support the feeble knees. Say to those who are of a fearful heart, "Be strong, fear not. Your God will come with vengeance, even God with a recompense; He will come and save you."'

God *was* saving me, and gradually building me up. Sure, I had fatigue, but no depression, no unhappiness. There was actually great joy in the midst of it all. When my body slowed down, I had to heed that. My wife sagely reminded me that my need to rest during these six weeks of treatment was an opportunity, not a restriction.

The fatigue wasn't from the treatment, but from a lack of continuous sleep. The ~~thermonuclear bombardment~~ radiotherapy had effectively frozen my bladder in place. It didn't work very well, so I was in and out of the loo about every hour. Things had slowed to a trickle. There was no longer a stream in the desert, you might say (pun intended).

This hourly need continued at night. All night, every night. Night after night. Instead of eight hours' sleep. I had eight to ten short naps. Even in the day I would only sleep for 45 minutes or so, just enough to dump me into REM sleep briefly and back out again. Much of the time I felt like I was floating. Other times I was trapped in Jell-O. I was mentally alert, but physically sluggish. I really was a piece of meat being tenderised for the grill.

PART THREE:

CONVICTION

19 December, 2019

My nights of short naps were interminable, with rock concerts full of dreams, and an unreality at night like I have never known. God was close, but it wasn't always a comfortable sensation. I woke up today fully tenderised and ready for cooking. Zechariah 4:6 was on my heart as soon as I was conscious. It's a famous verse that includes the well-known 'not by might, not by power, but by my Spirit, says the Lord of Hosts.' I read it and then read verse seven.

'Who are you, O great mountain? Before Zerubbabel you will be made level ground, and he will bring out the top stone amidst shouting of "Grace! Grace to the stone!"' This verse is a reflection of what the Faithful Pray-ers and Melanie and I have all been doing these many months. We've been proclaiming God's grace over the 'mountain' in my life.

When this all began in April, the tumour was the mountain. It was a natural thing that was *unnatural* to me, that is, unnatural to have in my body. But as the months went by, I came to understand that the real mountain in my life was actually a big pile of sin. There was a spiritual and emotional cancer in me that was literally eating me alive. My long-time 'Piss on it!' attitude became glaringly obvious to me, and it was ugly and despicable.

It was an attitude that had warped me and kept me from knowing true peace. Through all the physical challenges of cancer treatment I finished my first book, which was about how God healed me from the scars of childhood sexual abuse and all the sin (and redemption) that resulted from that. Together, God and I lanced that boil, squeezed the poison out and then He put on a bandage to protect the wound as He healed it.

That's how I had filled my days in 2019 when I wasn't snuggled into the chemotherapy easy chair or splayed out on the radiotherapy slab. It was spiritually and emotionally gruelling. The need for physical healing was merely a symptom of something deeper. 2019 was about healing my spirit more than about healing my body. As I stepped through the latter, God quietly worked on the former. And so, in the midst of all my fatigue and my extremely tenderised condition, I was ready to speak to the mountain, to *all* the mountains, visible and invisible.

A teaching I had on Zechariah 4:7 came to mind. It was a video of Joseph Prince, buried unlabelled somewhere on my laptop. I spent a half hour digging it out, and then watched it. To my surprise it said absolutely nothing to me. There was no message there for me at all! But the teaching wasn't the point. Holy Spirit had me sit through the symphony only for the coda.

Just as I moved to stop playback, it cut to something completely unrelated. The producers had added a clip where Prince led a congregation in communion. He held up the bread. 'Jesus said in John 6 that He is the bread of life. The life that He had to give to this world was His body.' In other words, Prince said, Jesus died so that I might live. He suffered so that I have health.

'So the more you partake (of communion),' Prince continued, 'the more life flows in your body. The more you partake, the stronger you become. God uses weak things to confound the mighty! God uses a piece of bread to put to nought that tumour in your body!'

WAIT! WHAT?? I'm really paying attention now.

He continued, holding the bread aloft. 'Hallelujah! This is the greatest radiation that there is!'

HOLD IT RIGHT THERE! I paused the video and went to get my own communion elements – the bread and the wine. I reversed it, and began again: 'God uses weak things to confound the mighty! God uses a piece of bread to put to nought that tumour in your body! Hallelujah! This is the greatest radiation that there is! This is the greatest antibiotic you can ever take!'

He concluded, 'Thank you, Lord Jesus. Surely in Your body, You have borne away all my diseases, all my sicknesses, all my pain, all my ageing, and by Your stripes, I am healed.' He paused and stared directly at me through the camera. 'Now tell the Lord what you are healed of.'

I held up the elements and shouted, *'BY YOUR STRIPES, I AM HEALED OF CANCER!'* and then took the bread, representing Christ's broken body that took on my tumour, and the wine, representing His shed blood that washed away my 'Piss on it!' attitude, and every other sin. My treatment would continue later in the day. But my healing was complete in that moment. God had killed the lie called cancer.

---

21 December, 2019

When you live a prophetic lifestyle, it's fair to say that you see things differently than many people. Certain things take on significance. I already mentioned the unexpected rearrangement of my radiotherapy schedule, so it ended the last day of the year – indeed the last day of the decade, a decade of tremendous spiritual transformation for me.

And so it was also of interest that my journal entry for 19 December, detailing the day I proclaimed *I AM HEALED*, filled the last three pages of my current notebook. I began a new journal the next day.

The first entry in it concerned the times and seasons described in Ecclesiastes chapter 3. I've been taught that if I see what season I'm in, for example, *'a time to kill and a time to heal'*, then I can better prepare myself to meet its current challenges.

I can also better prepare for the next season, which in that case would be *'a time to break down and a time to build up.'*

2019 had been a time to kill off some sinful thinking as well as the tumour in my bladder. It was a time also to heal, spiritually and physically. This is all a picture of how Christ's death and resurrection functioned, and my model for following Him. The killing came first and it looked like loss. But then followed healing and resurrection, ending in victory. This dying and coming back to life hadn't been easy for me, but the recipe for it was simple. Trust God, know He's good, do what's right, love mercy, and practice humility.* I was ready now to see how that goes, and do it with my new-found attitude.

---

24 December, 2019

I lay in the Linac machine for the 27th time. It was now decorated for Christmas. I stared at the cross of Christ in the ceiling. The cross was always directly in my line of vision each day of treatment. That reference cut-out on the ceiling represented more than just an image of the cross for me. It was prophetically important as well. In Radiotherapyland, the cut-out was that thing against which everything else was measured. It's exactly the same in God's terms. The cross is *that thing against which everything else is measured.* That ceiling tile is a powerful prophetic image for those who can accept it.

So I lay there, shorts pulled down, paper drape over my water works, picturing myself now as Isaac on the altar, a willing sacrifice. Abraham's faith was tested when God told him to sacrifice his son. As he and the boy headed for the

* Micah 6:8

mountain, Abraham told his servants to wait – that he and Isaac would go worship God and then 'be right back.'* Abraham had confidence God wouldn't allow the death of the son he and his wife Sarah had waited 25 years for.

Abraham had confidence in God's promises. After my experience the previous week, I finally did too. Doubt and fear were finally banished. In Isaac's case, he was tied to the altar of his father's faithful obedience. In my case, I was tied down to the altar of my *own* obedience, doing what God showed me was necessary for my healing.†

Or was it more than that? Was I the one on the cross instead? Was I actually being crucified with Christ? It was no longer me, myself. It was now about the Christ inside of me. My life was transforming into one of greater faith, from one of flesh. This was good. Flesh wears down, but faith continues eternally.‡

I was a veteran patient now, in my fifth week of treatment. Yet, when I came back to the suite today I forgot to void my bladder and had to be reminded. I told Helen I hoped it didn't jeopardize my status as 'Patient of the Year.' She responded with that caring and patient look I'd seen so many times before.

This business of being Patient of the Year was mostly an inside joke for myself. A reminder that whatever I do, I want to do with excellence. Even suffer. I asked the Faithful Pray-ers for prayers to strengthen my faith and my single-mindedness. *'Keep me strong and faithful to the end of this race, Lord, when You will be proven victorious once again.'*

---

* Genesis 22:5

† Consider Romans 12:1-2, especially the point about 'present your bodies as a living sacrifice'

‡ Galatians 2:20-21

31 December, 2019

It's the end of treatment. My final tanning session, number thirty-two. I have come to love all my technicians during our short time together, and will miss them. Helen, Temi, Martin, Katie, Raza, Christine, Sabrina, Dahlia, Luli, Kauser, Ellie, Karla, Fahmida, Anneka and more whose names I didn't catch.

Hidden Gems

The best things in life are always hidden in plain sight:
The knowing look,
A wild strawberry patch,
Tomorrow's plans.

That thing you couldn't find yesterday
Becomes tomorrow's old news.
What you do find in life is
Always in the last place you search.

Love, like water, finds its level.
Any crack in the wall becomes a flood.
My life is falling, falling toward You.
My heart is rising, rising toward You.

Perhaps I feel close to them because I was nearly naked in front of them every day, vulnerable, yet they made me comfortable. Or perhaps it was simply because they weren't jabbing needles in my arm and saying 'Sharp scratch!' But with all of them, those working the Chemotherapy Suites as well as the radiotherapy techs, there was a deep underlying kindness that was always visible. I thanked God for all of them.

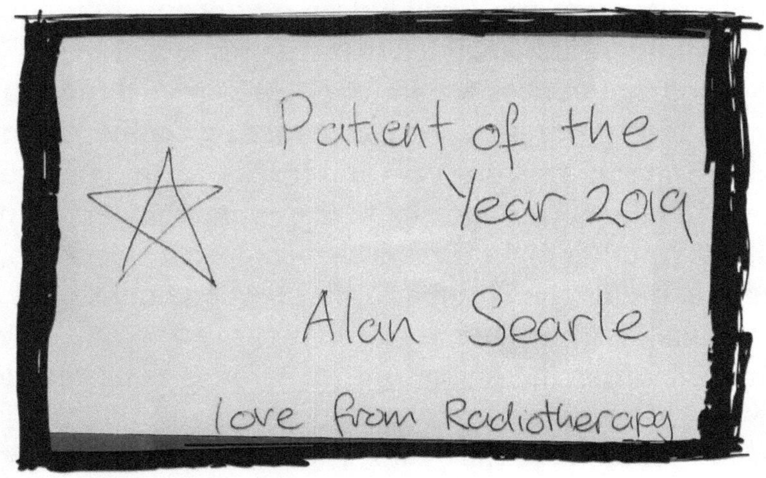

10 January, 2020

Rest and recovery. That's what my body needed now in the new year. A week and a half after radiotherapy my bladder thawed out. There was no pain, and the irritation that led to such frequent urination slowly abated. I began to sleep two hours at a time, and then three. My fatigue steadily vanished during a time when the doctors assured me I'd continue to worsen in both mind and body.

They didn't speak to my spiritual condition (not being trained for it), but that too was being reworked and healed. The sins I had confessed in the previous weeks led to repentance, a change of mind. That in turn allowed me to change long-standing attitudes into new ones. Repentance is good medicine. The unforgiving nature I carried out of my past life had led to a self-righteous heart, a heart lifted up on a pedestal. From that place, for too long, I had judged others and grown into a secretly intolerant man. It led to incredible restlessness.

My journal entries for January 2020 reveal night after night of intense dreams with a recurring theme: cleaning, washing myself, washing cars and trucks, running headlong through a rain storm. One night I was in the shower, trying to scrub off. Another night I was dream-trapped inside a washing machine. It was the Slumberland answer to my earlier cry from Psalm 51: 'Create in me a clean heart, O God, and renew a right spirit within me. Restore me to the joy of Your salvation...'

Night after night, God washed me clean of all the junk I'd accumulated over the years. Then in the day, there was a burning fire. He used 'the greatest radiation that there is' – the Holy Spirit – to burn the wrongness out of me, as I continued to pray and reflect. From the ashes of that burning rose a man living in concert with the identity God gave him. After that, my anxiety disappeared.

---

22 January, 2020 (home)

'You will spring to new life.' I finally understood that this message was not just about renewing my body. It was about renewing my spirit. That verse in Revelation I saw back on 3 December came back to mind. It was Jesus speaking. 'I was dead, but now look – I am alive forever and ever. And I hold the keys that unlock death and the unseen world. Now I want you to write what you have seen...'*

* Revelation 1:18-19 (TPT)

And so, on 22 January, I was given the idea to write this book, writing what I have seen, and feared, and felt, and thought, and lived. I would finish the story before my meeting with the doctors to review my post-treatment scans. Then I'd come home, write the last bit, and be done.

I knew the lie called cancer was dead. God proclaimed it dead that day in December when I celebrated communion. My healing had come then, and I wanted the doctors to know what God had done *before* they had their own proofs. That way God gets the glory He deserves. Put another way, I needed to write for the record before writing for the world.

---

22 January, 2020 (NHS)

Patient Statement - Please place in my medical file
Alan Searle
22/01/2020

I was given a diagnosis of bladder cancer in the spring of 2019 and had a portion of a tumour surgically removed on 4 June, 2019. From July through September I received four rounds of chemotherapy (Gem-Cis) and then 32 radiotherapy treatments (with seven weekly infusions of Cisplatin) in November and December 2019.

During the entire period, from my first presentation of symptoms in April 2019 I received regular and ongoing prayer in the name of Jesus Christ at the Healing Rooms of SW London, at my church, Holy Trinity Clapham, and from a group of friends in the UK, Europe and America.

I believe this prayer strengthened my body's rejection of any cancer, strengthened my immune system, and beat back the normal level of side-effects from treatment.

Dr. (Brio) and others on the Urology Team remarked repeatedly at my overall level of health during treatment and my lack of symptom presentation. Dr. (Brio) repeatedly referred to me as a 'poster boy' for maintaining health through radiotherapy.

Although I experienced a moderate level of constipation during the first of my four rounds of chemotherapy, these conditions abated quickly and disappeared almost completely while I was awaiting radiotherapy. Most of this I believe was not from the chemotherapy drug but from the anti-sickness medication. When I stopped taking it voluntarily, the constipation ceased. I had no nausea or sickness during chemotherapy. My appetite was excellent and I lost no weight.

My experience of radiotherapy was not at all what was predicted either. I did experience some fatigue in the second week, mostly due to nocturia and several nights of eight one-hour naps rather than complete nights of sleep. Other than that, radiotherapy was not a burden and did not greatly affect my day-to-day life. I was able to work regularly (I work at home) and complete an 18-month writing project.

I had very little diarrhoea and no loss of appetite, and no weight loss during radiotherapy. In the first week of radiotherapy treatment I was able to run from the front door of Guy's Cancer-Free Centre to the top of the escalators at London Bridge Station and catch my breath by the time I walked to the end of Platform 13 to get my train.

Dr. (Brio) indicted that I would likely feel increasingly fatigued in the weeks after radiotherapy ended 31 December 2019, but this was

not the case either. On 15 January 2020 I sprinted flat-out for more than 100 metres to catch a bus and was not seriously winded.

My urinary pattern has returned to normal as of this date and my sleep pattern is almost back to what it was before treatment began.

I will say for the record that I received a very strong sense during a prayer session of my own on 19 December that I was healed as of that day, and indeed in the days following that, any remaining symptoms began to abate, even as radiotherapy continued. It is my firm belief that I am currently cancer free and that the scans to be performed in 2020 will bear this out.

(s) Alan Searle

---

22 February 2020

A full month flew by as this manuscript lengthened. Healing continued to be less about my body and more about my soul. Even as my body recovered, my spirit continued to be worked over, but it was uplifting now. Being pounded down into the dirt by cancer treatment had left me more than physically flat. It had also emptied me spiritually. But that was weeks ago.

Empty had been good. I was like a lump of clay then, unable to hold anything. Like a potter works his lump, God had worked on me. The clay spun on the wheel and under expert hands, the sides rose, and an interior was pinched out, a place to hold something. As the potter continued to work, the clay turned from a lump into a pot. Its interior grew and it held a little bit, then more, and then much more.

Back in December, before the breakthrough moment when I confidently shouted, '*I AM HEALED OF CANCER!*', I'd been backed into a spiritual corner. What I thought I knew about divine healing didn't match my own experience. I'd seen miraculous things happen through healing prayer. When it didn't happen for me, it led to that 'why me' moment. Here's the deal: I've seen God show up and perform miracles and I selfishly and arrogantly wanted one for myself. I forgot there is no second-class healing.

There was a time in early 2018 when I prayed for a woman, and then watched the power of God make a patch of psoriasis disappear right under my own hands. It was a rough scaly patch about the size of my palm. She had it on her right shin since a missionary trip in Africa several years before.

The team and I prayed and I believed strongly that I should lay hands on the patch itself, which I did with her permission. As we prayed, I something like heat radiated from my palm and the patch just shrunk. It was almost like a movie special effect, and I was blown away. The fresh skin that now matched the rest of her leg changed my thinking and vastly built my faith in that moment.

Also that same year I was on a team that prayed for a severely injured dancer, and then watched her easily jump up and down with no pain after being touched by God. These experiences, and others, proved to me that God heals directly through prayer. So, why not me? I can't answer that.

All the faith I and others mustered didn't wipe away my tumour, even if it did abate the side-effects of treatment. I got to walk the difficult road of chemotherapy and radiation instead. Then, almost at the end of that road, twelve days before the end of my treatment, God delivered to me the certainty that He had healed me.

I found that walking that hard road built my faith also, in ways I hadn't anticipated. Why? On reflection, It's because

I had to work at it. God wasn't always present to me, and there were days I really had to search for Him. Sometimes, I couldn't find Him. It was hard, but so is pursuing anything with abandon.

---

13 March, 2020

I began writing this account in early February 2020, reviewing the previous 10 months. Now, five weeks later, the review is complete, and the rest of this book is 'as it happens,' contemporaneous. It's a journal now, not a historical review. As I wait out the weeks until I can be scanned, reviewed and released, I watch a new virus sweep across the world. At this point it's unknown how bad it will be, and people are afraid.

I'm an intercessor, so I pray. *Prayer is warfare,* and I must be well-armed. I won't stay unprotected on the battlefield. Prayer remains my front-line weapon, as it has been throughout my Cancer-Free year. My prayer is often wrapped up inside the Scripture I read. I go through the Bible, a bit most every day, from beginning to end on an on-going basis. When I get to the end of Revelation, I begin again 'in the beginning,' where God created the heavens and the earth.

Today I'm reading the book of Jeremiah, which is appropriate, considering the state of the world. Jeremiah did a lot of lamenting, as you may know. He wasn't known as the Laughing Prophet, after all. Anyway, he wrote this: '"The harvest has finished, and the summer is gone," the people cry, "yet we are not saved!"'*

---

* Jeremiah 8:20

My NLT Study Bible says the people simply gave up instead of confessing their sin and asking God for help. The harvest time referred to was their own salvation, but they missed it. I faced that same decision at the beginning of my Cancer-Free year. Do I turn to God, or away from Him?

Begging God for things doesn't work. That's what Jeremiah warned the people of Judah, and what he warns me about today. If I want God's attention, I have to repent (change my thinking) and confess my mistakes. That not only gets God's attention, it also turns away evil, if I do these things in a timely way.* It seems I had.

So here I am, with this brushfire of a virus beginning to sweep across the world. Will it take more dead wood out of my heart? That is, will I continue to rethink how I live? Or, will I just ride it out, hoping for the best? As fear and anxiety mount here in the UK, we appear to be careening toward a lock-down of some sort. That would be an opportunity for serious self-examination to continue. The time of picking through my personal trash may not be over.

If life becomes more difficult from coronavirus, I can drift along and simply comfort myself, or I can apply myself to understand what God promises to 'those who fear him' (that means those who worship Him – not those who wrongly think He can't wait to be punitive).

Running toward Him worked for me during diagnosis and surgery. It worked well during chemotherapy, even when I was in the depths of despair. It worked so well during radiotherapy that I was lifted up and, finally, divinely healed. It works now as I wait for late April, when the doctors will catch up with God's diagnosis. And it will work in any oppressive days to come.

* This is shown most dramatically in the book of Jonah. Jonah is told to warn Nineveh, capital of arguably the most evil and cruel empire of its day. Surprisingly, they do repent, and fast, from the king all the way down to the lowliest draft animal. God relents, and Assyria is left alone for another 100 years.

Don't misunderstand; I'm human. Every time I approach God's 'Trust Me' cliff, I *always* look down dizzily and gulp. I can never see the bottom. And when I finally have courage enough to jump – expecting to fall – I land in his invisible, outstretched hand, softly, safely. He hides the wisdom of his landing pad. I can only find it by jumping. It's always an act of faith. It's the only way life truly works.

---

24 March, 2020 – Lock-down, Day One

As I race to the end of this memoir during the Great Coronavirus Freak-out of 2020, the NHS has classified me as a Vulnerable Adult. I believe I'm 100% healed and my immune system is as good as ever, so I'm clapped in irony as much as in irons. This is day one of a mandatory 12-week ~~house arrest~~ self-isolation. Instead of being free to go about my business while I await my final scans next month, I'm now ~~behind bars~~ told to stay in a benign location.

My daughter Brenna told me I should not be surprised. 'On paper, you should be (considered vulnerable). Age over 60, recently off chemo- and radiotherapies, history of excessive vice. Medical experts don't account for spiritual healing, for better or worse,' she said. Yeah, yeah. No matter that even during chemotherapy Melanie got sick twice while I didn't rate a sniffle. I don't even get to complain. Instead, I got a text:

NHS CORONAVIRUS SERVICE: We have identified that you're someone at risk of severe illness if you catch Coronavirus. Please remain at home for a minimum of 12 weeks. Home is the safest *place for you. Staying in helps you stay well and that will help the NHS too. You can open a window, but do not leave your home.*[*]

(Insert sanctimonious Christian grumble here)

On the other hand, I now rate preferential treatment for home delivery slots from my local supermarket and pharmacy. I'd rather go out and stand in a queue, an extravert's delight. God bless the NHS anyway for their care, even if they haven't caught up with my reality.

---

26 March, 2020 – Lock-down, Day Three

Being on lock-down is nothing less than a reinforcement of the most important lesson learned during my Cancer-Free year. What is it? Turn away from the false gods that I love so well, so that when I'm out of ~~house arrest~~ self-isolation I'll have no desire for them any more. My false gods, my idols, are falling on their faces one by one.

It's like a story in the first book of Samuel. The Philistines had captured the Ark of the Covenant, which Israel had brought out onto the battlefield. But the Philistines made the mistake of setting the ark in the temple of their god, Dagon. 'And when the people of Ashdod arose early in the morning, there was Dagon, fallen on its face to the earth before the ark of the Lord.'[†]

They stood Dagon back up again and the next morning they not only found it face-down in front of the ark, but with its head and both its hands cut off. That's what's happening here in my room as I sit alone with God. One by one my idols

* That last clause obviously added to prevent me from suicidally pitching to my death from despair.

† 1 Sam 5:3 (NKJV)

crash to the floor, heads and hands torn asunder. They fade to insignificance in the face of a God who heals, a God who loves, a God who restores.

These false gods cannot rise again of their own accord. The critical question is whether I'll be short-sighted enough to stand them up again when this is all over. Or will I leave them earthbound, where they belong?

---

8 April, 2020 – Lock-down, Day 16

I've been advised by Guy's Hospital that staff are '*working hard to respond to the current coronavirus situation, and many appointments will be cancelled, moved to a different location or changed to a telephone call.*'

Also, from NHS: '*NHS England have written to your hospital to ask them to review any ongoing care that you have with them. It is possible that some clinics and appointments will be cancelled or postponed. Your hospital or clinic will contact you if any changes need to be made to your care or treatment. Otherwise you should assume your care or treatment is taking place as planned.*'

Just in case, I called the Urology Centre and they confirmed the dates and times for my scans. I'm also still on track to meet with the doctor on 24 April. What's even better is that I may receive a bonus cystoscopy at no extra charge! I keep telling myself that it's One Of My Favourite Things, but that Sound of Music number is not playing out. Oh well, an internal exam, uncomfortable though it be, is a small price to pay for them to see what I've known since 19 December: I'm healed. I'm completely healed.

16 April, 2020 – Lock-down, Day 24

This is the most excitement I've had in almost a month. I get to travel all the way to Guy's today after more than three weeks of ~~sensory deprivation~~ near isolation. Today's scans will verify to the medical team that I'm clean of cancer, and I'm excited about that.

It's a lovely spring day. Being out and about is restorative. It's the time of year that's a flower lover's dream and an allergy sufferer's bane. Train travel to London Bridge Station is unremarkable if unusual. Walking to the railway station there are no open shops, no children being walked by parents to school. Only one or two vehicles pass me on the roadway, instead of a steady stream of bikes, cars and lorries.

There are still four trains per hour headed to London Bridge Station, but they only have half the usual number of coaches. The coach I enter will seat four dozen, and normally would be half-full. There are two other people in it. The journey is and isn't like so many I've made before. Another difference appears in the form of a human barrier at the Cancer-Free Centre entrance. I was quizzed about my health and then given a mask, which I'm encouraged to keep on, and directed to use the hand sanitiser.

My time at the Cancer-Free Centre involved a CT scan, followed by yet another blood sample. Then I moved over to the main hospital for an MRI. Both scans involve disrobing of course. At the Cancer-Free Centre, you may recall, all my goods are stuffed in a plastic basket. At the main hospital MRI suite, they go in a locker. That gives them control over what gets close to the big magnet in the MRI machine.

The locker key and the door to the changing room have green tape on them reading CLEAN. I resisted taking a strip of it home as a prophetic act, to proclaim that these scans would prove to the medical team that my body is clean of cancer. Interestingly, after I was home, I was shuffling through some papers that I thought might hold yet another nugget for this book. As I did, I found a forgotten I AM CLEAN sticker purloined months ago. As I pasted it in my journal alongside the first one I heard this: 'You have sprung to new life.'

---

17 April, 2020 – Lock-down, Day 25

The phone rang about 10.30 this morning. It was Brio, although I wasn't supposed to hear from him for another week. I put him on speaker.

'I have great news!' he said. 'Your scans looked absolutely fine. There's no evidence of any cancer on your scans.'

Whoops, applause, thanks to God at the Searle end of the line. He did tell us there appeared to be a bit of scarring where the tumour had been, which they'll look at next Friday with the cystoscope. And then in three more months, another MRI and more blood work to check my kidney function.

'Otherwise, it all looks fantastic,' he continued, 'The CT scan is very good at looking outside the bladder but looking inside the bladder (with the MRI) it all looks pristine as well.'

The truly important news to me was, 'Your immune system is just fine.' I may not be invulnerable, but I'm no longer considered 'vulnerable.' I'm finally free to wander about the planet within government guidelines. We hung up the phone and launched into a praise party. Not so much because of the news itself, but because it officially brought the matter to a close.

Frankly, the scan results were a bit of an anti-climax, because I was already assured of the outcome. But the validation of what God had said, and done, was glorious news to share.

PART FOUR:

SENTENCE

18 April, 2020

Today is exactly one year from the day my life changed suddenly and radically in a South London men's room. If that day was the first day of my year on trial, the day of Dr. Brio's call – yesterday – was the last. It was a 365 day stretch that changed me physically, emotionally and, most important, spiritually.

The revelation that I had a bloody malignant tumour eating away at the wall of my bladder arrested my life. Normal living came to a complete halt. I was forced by circumstance to cease taking the long view. I began living day by day. Sometimes, it was hour by hour. On more than a few occasions, it was minute by minute. There was no making of plans. And the plans we had made before all this began, for our trips to Bradford and Cornwall, only played out because of God's generosity.

Treatment for cancer put me on trial in all areas of my life. The physical nature of it was harsh sometimes, but pain, and its sibling, grief, can be borne. I asked for grace, and (mostly) carried on with joy. In her allegory, Hinds' Feet in High Places, Hannah Hurnard's protagonist, Much-Afraid, finds a tiny flower growing in the desert where no flower should be. The flower tells her its name is Acceptance-With-Joy.

Much-Afraid says to herself about her Shepherd, 'He has brought me here when I did not want to come, for his own purpose.' I related to that. Reflecting on her own journey of faith, Much-Afraid also names herself 'Acceptance-With-Joy.' Can I do any less?

I had been taken to spiritual places I did not want to go. My physical trial, like Much-Afraid's, was about accepting my pain, and my circumstance, and through that, my sin. I'd like to say I bore the physical part of it well, with relatively few moments where my bodily condition got the better of me. The spiritual portion of the trial was much more difficult. I might find losing a limb easier to bear than laying down my pride. But until I did that, until I leapt into the unknown and trusted my own heavenly Shepherd, I remained in great spiritual pain.

When I need to be humbled, I have only two choices, my way or God's way. When I do things His way, I have to begin by humbling myself. When I do things my way, I end up being humiliated. Guess which I prefer? My trial is over. I've been convicted of my sins. I was found not guilty, because I asked to be forgiven. And when God forgives, it's a life sentence. I am sentenced to everlasting life.

---

23 April, 2020

If you read this book hoping for some Hollywood-esque flash-bang miracle, sorry to disappoint. If you wanted absolute undeniable proof that God healed me divinely with no human aid, too bad. What you have instead is a story about my *belief* of His hand in my healing, and the signs and wonders accompanying His word about it. I report; you decide.

I know God was involved in my healing, and all the prayer I received contributed to my happy outcome. It created an atmosphere where faith and hope ruled, not fear. It created an atmosphere where my spirit was open to His Spirit, to that 'still small voice'* that I daily strain to hear amidst the roar of doubt and the din of anxiety.

Evangelist A. W. Tozer said, 'I may not be able to explain it, but I definitely know when the Holy Spirit speaks to me, and that is the time for me to stop whatever I am doing and listen.'

* 1 Kings 19:12

I had stopped and listened a lot during my year on trial. It was vital, to retain my faith, strengthen my hope, and carry His joy. I gained some wisdom during my Cancer-Free year, and I hope you get something from reading about it.

The connections I make in this story between what I believe God did, and my current state of health are correlative, not causative. Thus, The Lie Called Cancer is purely a story about faith, not about proofs. God doesn't work by proving Himself to me if I don't see His work through my faith.

The only proof God needs to give is His existence. He won't stoop to my level and provide some demonstration that I might demand. The Gospel accounts of Jesus' interactions with religious authority shout this truth. The Pharisees stumbled repeatedly over their own demands, trying to avoid Jesus' truth.

Most of what I know about God and how He works is circumstantial. It's full of assumptions, even if confident ones. However, there is one thing I do know well, having learnt it the hard way. That is that God wants me to act in faith. Fortunately, I had learned this before my Cancer-Free year. In this way I knew it was imperative to surrender my 'right to know' in favour of His right to answer in His own time. When He does answer, it's always *after* I act in faith. Then, and only then, do the proofs arrive. Insisting on having it the other way around is like demanding heat from a fire before striking the match.

The first time I risked striking the match of faith years ago, the fire's heat was miraculous. Now, years later, I'm certain the heat will always come. But sometimes I'm still afraid to strike the match. In this story, that was my long refusal to surrender to the possibility of surgery. My refusal to jump off the cliff-edge of faith. It's easy to point out these mistakes in retrospect. In the heat of battle, mistakes are always made. Fortunately, I serve a God who's willing to forgive me when I fess up after making them.

Nicholas Herman, a 17th century Carmelite monk known as Brother Lawrence, wrote a timeless classic on The Practice of the Presence of God. In it, he suggests that God permits diseases of the body to cure those of the soul. It refines us to rely on Him through life's trials and come out the other side, he says. Brother Lawrence wrote, 'The difficulties of life do not have to be unbearable. It is the way we look at them – through faith or unbelief – that makes them seem so.'

And so it is for me. Because I chose the way of faith, I walk free and shall be healed, in all ways.

PART FIVE:

WALKING FREE

1 May, 2020

Here are a few afterthoughts. I had to undertake some serious repentance after writing that stuff about being on house arrest and behind bars during my 25 days of 'self-isolation' as a 'vulnerable adult.' My thinking was all wrong. My mindset had me <u>*counting down to freedom.*</u> My eyes were set on the day when I would no longer be confined to my home.

But what makes my freedom, really? Is it merely measured by my ability to come and go as I wish? Do I define it only by an untrammelled lifestyle? No, there's much more to it than that. What hauled me up short was the reminder that <u>*I am not my own*</u>. When I gave my life to Christ, I set myself at His bidding and I look to Him for my freedom. And here I was reducing it all to a measurement of whether I was allowed to leave my flat.

Sometimes my joking nature takes me beyond the desire to just 'look at the bright side.' This is another thing learned in my Cancer-Free year, that I'm wrong to dumb down my definition of freedom to something mundane, and make it dependent on life's conditions. During the darkest days of my treatment I believed my freedom was dependent on how I felt physically. That was wrong. Freedom is an entirely spiritual matter, which I have just learned the hard way.

A classic verse about this says, 'For freedom Christ freed us. Stand fast therefore and do not be entangled again with the yoke of bondage.'* In other words, if my freedom comes from a surrender to Christ, I can hold onto it wherever I am and whatever I'm doing. It depends on Him, not on me, not on

---

* Galatians 5:1 TPT

how I feel. That 'yoke of bondage' there – well, that's my desire to make it all about me.

Social media memes during the coronavirus lock-down tried to be profound about freedom but they failed. So what if Paul wrote half the New Testament while under house arrest? Does it really matter that Newton did groundbreaking work while 'self-isolating' from the plague? These observations miss the point.

Their focus is wrongly on *doing*, which is where I prop up my idols. I need to focus first on *being*. Only then will my *doing* be well-anchored and sensible. God didn't call me to a life of *doing* to earn His love. He called me to a state of *being* in love with Him. It's a relationship designed to stir my heart and motivate me to *then* get busy and do.

God calls me to take action out of love, not just be someone who loves to take action. I find total freedom in the former and hardly any freedom in the latter. Understanding freedom was another important lesson from my Cancer-Free year. The Bible says 'Don't view this wonderful freedom as an opportunity to set up a base of operations in the natural realm. Freedom means that we become so completely free of self-indulgence that we become servants of one another, expressing love in all we do.'*

I stopped counting the days to 'freedom'. That counting leaves me 'setting up a base of operations'. Like the prisoner marking the days on the wall, I'd be hunkered in my bunker, waiting to be let out. The truth is that I was released from prison and given freedom the day I was born again. I have my freedom today. The only question left is, what shall I do with it?

---

* Galatians 5:13 (TPT)

24 May, 2020

As mentioned frequently, Isaiah 35 was my cane when I was weak, and a steadying hand to the elbow when I couldn't move forward during my Cancer-Free year. It brought life when death loomed, and completed a picture for me of how God answers prayer. Melanie and I had already moved into reliance on prayer before God showed me the riches in this passage in early July, 2019. We had struck the match of faith early – back in May – and His heat came, as we knew it would.

Isaiah 35 is superficially about the future glory of Zion, God's permanent capital. But at my personal level, it's about hope for restoration and revival. In these verses, Isaiah offers a prophetic picture of God's promise to answer when we cry for help. Then, when He comes in response to prayer, miracles happen.

Jesus promised this when He taught the prayer recorded in Matthew 6:10: 'Your kingdom come; Your will be done on earth, as it is in heaven.' I cried out to God repeatedly in this way during my Cancer-Free year. As you have witnessed, He answered.

> 1 The wilderness and the solitary place shall be glad,
> and the desert shall rejoice and blossom as the rose;
> 2 it shall blossom abundantly and rejoice even with joy
> and singing. The glory of Lebanon shall be given to it,
> the excellency of Carmel and Sharon. They shall see the
> glory of the Lord and the excellency of our God.

The overwhelming nature of God's promises are shown in the superlatives found in the first two verses: glad, rejoice, blossom abundantly, joy and singing, glory, excellency. These are reliable even in our greatest times of spiritual barrenness.

> 3 Strengthen the weak hands, and support the feeble
> knees. 4 Say to those who are of a fearful heart, "Be strong,

> fear not. Your God will come with vengeance, even God with a recompense; He will come and save you."

God comes to those who are obedient and faithful, and who cry out to Him, even from a place of desperation or fear.

> 5 Then the eyes of the blind shall be opened, and the
> ears of the deaf shall be unstopped. 6 Then the lame man
> shall leap as a deer, and the tongue of the mute sing for
> joy. For in the wilderness waters shall break out and
> streams in the desert.

'Then' shows that the healing that happens next is a result of our obedience and faithful prayer. After He comes, then the eyes of the blind and the ears of the deaf are opened, then the lame walk and the mute speak, then the lie called cancer is dispelled. These verses also show that God is not just a Healer, but also heals us beyond what we ask for. The mute may wish to speak, but He also has them sing! The lame may wish to walk – He also has them leap!

In my spiritual wilderness, when I needed a drink, He brought an oasis, He came to me and said, 'You will spring to new life.' He always thinks bigger than I do.

> 7 The parched ground shall become a pool, and the thirsty land springs of water; in the habitation of jackals where each lay, there shall be grass with reeds and rushes.

The word translated 'jackals' is the Hebrew word tannîym, which is doubled in the text for emphasis. It's often translated as 'dragon', which of course is symbolically the devil. In this passage, God transforms a place where only hideous creatures will dwell into one full of gentility and life.

> 8 A highway shall be there, a roadway, and it shall be called the Highway of Holiness. The unclean shall not

> pass on it, but it shall be for the wayfaring men, and fools shall not wander on it.'

'Highway' here does means a thoroughfare for travel, but the word translated as 'roadway' is the Hebrew derek, which means a course of action, or what we might today call a lifestyle. The wayfaring men are those who choose this path to salvation that God has offered. They set out on it in obedience, not knowing their destination, but trusting that it is good.

> 9 No lion shall be there, nor any ravenous beast shall
> go up on it; these shall not be found there, but the
> redeemed shall walk there, 10 and the ransomed of the
> Lord shall return and come to Zion with songs and
> everlasting joy upon their heads. They shall obtain joy
> and gladness, and sorrow and sighing shall flee away.

I'm one of those 'ransomed of the Lord.' When Jesus died on the cross and paid the price for my sin, He bought the rights to my life (and yours). The passage ends with the greatest news of all, that in the end I'll return to God, meaning I'll repent of my wrongdoing and turn back (Hebrew shoob) to God, who will be waiting with open arms to restore (Hebrew shoob) me.

Chapter 12 of the book of Hebrews offers a plain-spoken New Testament parallel to this: 'Now all discipline seems to be more pain than pleasure at the time, yet later it will produce a transformation of character, bringing a harvest of righteousness and peace to those who yield to it. So be made strong even in your weakness by lifting up your tired hands in prayer and worship. And strengthen your weak knees, for as you keep walking forward on God's paths all your stumbling ways will be divinely healed!'

To which I say, 'So be it!'

25 May, 2020

You finished the book! Congratulations!

Now you can take my suggestion from *How to Use This Book* and visit my website, *Pleasant Lines* (https://alansearle.media), where you can sign up for my newsletter. That gives you Insider status with access to periodic non-spam-like communication, free stuff, and maybe some teasers about what I'm writing next.

Or you can hang out there and read *Alan Says* which is my take on what's happening around us.

You can double your pleasure by following my Facebook feed at https://facebook.com/PleasantLinesWriter.

I'm worth reading, just like the Bible.

Acknowledgements

Many thanks to the leadership at Holy Trinity Clapham for encouraging a culture of prayer and worship, and for the leaders and elders at Oasis Church, Colliers Grove, which hosts the Healing Rooms of SW London.

I'm grateful to my thousands of chauffeurs at Transport for London and Britain's rail services, who are constantly at my beck and call. You move machinery from Point A to Point B with great dispatch and attention to safety, and made all my commutes pleasant.

Thanks to my daughter Rachel Richards for unknowingly providing graphic imagery that I took without asking permission.

I offer a gentlemanly bow to Teddi Black and Megan McCullough for their excellence in the presentation of this book. May God continue to prosper the work of your hands.

My wife Melanie Searle deserves all praise for ~~enduring~~ loving and supporting me through the lie called cancer, and through the fallout of my decision to write about it. She's exceedingly gracious to occasionally appear in print for comic effect. I love her deeply, and not just for that.

I can exclusively reveal, Melanie, that your critique of this book while it was still a work-in-progress improved it immeasurably. As my brother Newell famously said, 'There are no great writers. There are only great editors.' You are an exemplar of the Proverbs 31 woman. I'm boyishly excited about the many years to come.

At various points in the text I profusely thanked the staffs at Kings College Hospital, London, at Guy's Hospital London, especially its Urology Centre and the Aston Keys Ward, and at Guy's Cancer-Free Centre. Your skill, care and dedication is without peer. You are diligent and modest while doing the work of angels. Thank you for loving me so well.

Finally, I can only blow a virtual kiss (at arm's length, from behind bulletproof Lexan) to Angel #2. I'm simply afraid to come any closer to you, sister.

About the Cover

Teddi Black's striking cover design reflects one of my favourite stories in which the Old Testament points forward to the life of Jesus. It's about Jesus' fulfilment of Israel's prophetic history. It's from the Book of Numbers, that story of Israel's four-decade walkabout in the wilderness. Despite being lifted miraculously out of slavery and being fed and watered endlessly, these people stupidly began grumbling for the thousandth time how much they hated it.

'So the Lord sent poisonous serpents among the people, and they bit the people, and many children of Israel died.' The people then ran to Moses and pleaded for help, after they realised their 'Piss on it!' attitude was a sin. Moses 'prayed for the people'.

What does God have Moses do to save them? Did He have Moses bless the people? Pray for them? No. Concoct a holy elixer? No. Did He have someone run through the crowd with incense to make atonement like He did the previous time they were whining? No.

He had Moses make a bronze serpent and put it on a pole, and 'if a serpent had bitten any man, when he looked at the bronze serpent he lived.'*

The bronze serpent was a prophetic image of the Messiah. I know, that's very weird, although the symbolism is sweeping. The serpent was the tempter that introduced sin into the world in the Garden of Eden. The serpent thus becomes a symbol for sin. So why would the Israelites be healed by gazing on a visual representation of sin? It was a prophecy of Christ.

* You'll find the story of the bronze serpent in Numbers 21. The story about the people being protected by incense is in Numbers 16. The Israelites grumbled a lot, and as a result all but two of the million or so who left Egypt died in the desert. We can all learn from that, I think.

You and I are healed (receive our salvation) by gazing on Christ, only we get to see the *post-crucifixion Christ*. Jesus lived a perfect life and then died as a sacrifice for our sin: mine, yours and everyone's. So when we consider Him (gaze upon Him, call upon Him), we are healed. We are saved.

Jesus told the great Jewish teacher Nicodemus, 'Just as Moses lifted up the serpent in the wilderness, even so must the Son of Man be lifted up, that whoever believes in Him should not perish, but may have eternal life.'*

Did you get that? If that wasn't enough, try this promise: 'Everyone who calls on the name of the Lord shall be saved.'† It's that easy, and that simple. Next time you're in trouble, say 'Jesus, help!' and mean it. And see what happens.

Huh, Maybe I *can* evangelise in a book of this type.

---

* John 3:14-15
† Romans 10:13

A Personal Note to You

The Bible is the most published, most loved, most feared and most hated book ever written. Probably because it's from God, and He always freaks us out. For a simple way to get into the Bible, please visit and support The Bible Project, https://bibleproject.com/ which has accessible fun videos worth watching. Yes, the Bible is fun. Especially the stranger things...

www.ingramcontent.com/pod-product-compliance
Lightning Source LLC
Chambersburg PA
CBHW030924060726
47591CB00005B/1655

9781838044619